# Compared to What?

# Compared to What?

## ON WRITING AND THE WRITER'S LIFE

## THOMAS FARBER

W · W · Norton & Company

New York    London

Copyright © 1988 by Thomas Farber
All rights reserved.
Published simultaneously in Canada by Penguin Books Canada Ltd.,
2801 John Street, Markham, Ontario L3R 1B4.
Printed in the United States of America.
The text of this book is composed in 11/13 Goudy Old Style,
with display type set in Goudy Old Style.
Composition and manufacturing by the Maple-Vail Book Manufacturing Group.
Book design by Margaret M. Wagner.
First Edition

Library of Congress Cataloging-in-Publication Data
Farber, Thomas, 1944–
    Compared to what? : on writing and the writer's life / Thomas
Farber, — 1st ed.
      p.  cm.
    1. Farber, Thomas, 1944–    —Biography. 2. Authors,
American—20th century—Biography.  3. Authorship.  I. Title.
PS3556.A64Z465 1988
813'.54—dc19                                                  88-10017
[B]
ISBN 0-393-02611-6

W. W. Norton & Company, Inc. 500 Fifth Avenue, New York, N. Y. 10110
W. W. Norton & Company Ltd. 37 Great Russell Street, London WC1B 3NU
1 2 3 4 5 6 7 8 9 0

# PERMISSIONS

Excerpt from *Façade* reprinted from *The Collected Poems* of Edith Sitwell by permission of the publisher, Vanguard Press, Inc. © 1968 by Vanguard Press, Inc. © 1949, 1953, 1954, 1959, 1962, 1963 by Dame Edith Sitwell.

"This Be the Verse" from *High Windows* by Philip Larkin. Copyright © 1974 by Philip Larkin. Reprinted by permission of Farrar, Straus and Giroux, Inc.

Excerpts from "The Circus Animals' Desertion" and "What Then." Reprinted with permission of Macmillan Publishing Company from *Collected Poems* by W. B. Yeats. Copyright 1940 by Georgie Yeats, renewed 1968 by Bertha Georgie Yeats, Michael Butler Yeats and Anne Yeats.

Excerpt from "The Dolphin" from *The Dolphin* by Robert Lowell. Copyright © 1973 by Robert Lowell. Reprinted by permission of Farrar, Straus and Giroux, Inc.

Lines from "Slow Hand" by Michael Clark and John Bettis. © 1980 Sweet Harmony Music, Warner-Tamerlane Publishing Corp. & Flying Dutchman Music    All Rights Reserved    Used by Permission

The first draft of this book was defined in part at the Rockefeller Foundation's Villa Serbelloni at Bellagio, Italy. The author also once again gives special thanks to W.B.G.

One section of this text appeared earlier in somewhat different form as a chapbook from Peter B. Howard/ Serendipity Books, Poltroon Press, printer.

For ELLEN, STEVE, and MIMI—also *Left-Behind*— and for HSU YIN PEH

# Compared to What?

THE writer was back in Boston yet one more time, and again it was summer. The year before, he and Mad Dog had played pickup basketball down by the Charles. Near Harvard, just off Memorial Drive at Dunster House. It must have been a hundred that day, humidity right up there. Foliage imitating Henri Rousseau. *Psychedelic,* as they used to say. Oh, those poor Pilgrims, starving and shivering that first desperate winter with Squanto et al., only to be sweating it out by July.

The writer and Mad Dog were both in fine fettle, each back from somewhere, pleased to return to terra cognita. They were playing well too, always a comfort. Running hard, bantering, applause for anyone's good move. The other players were blacks from the neighborhood. There's Harvard, some blue-collar families, the students and professionals who love Cambridgeport, a few remaining bohemians and folkies (Richard Fariña / Jim Kweskin / Mimi Baez lived here), and then—poof!—a small ghetto. After one game, a player asked the writer, "Say, where do you and the redhaired guy know each other from?" Earlier, on one of his lumbering drives to the hoop, the writer and this man had collided. "Your chin fouled my elbow," the writer had said after the impact. Now, answering the question, he responded, "Mad Dog? Where do we know each other from? We met on Death Row." Hearing this, Mad Dog began to laugh—"like a bastard," to use his idiom—and then took off around the corner to the local minimart for a six-pack.

Later that afternoon, Mad Dog saw two small black children tussling near the sandbox on the far side of the court. Pulling them apart, he picked up the one who'd been losing. So there was Mad Dog, nose bulbous, capillaries cracked from too many whiskies, Budweiser for breath, face right in the kid's. The writer thought of the convict in *Great Expectations*—Magwitch?—jumping out from behind the gravestone, scaring Pip to death. Here, however, was this three-year-old black child up in Mad Dog's powerful Irish arms. "What's your name?" Mad Dog asked in a gruff voice. Mock gruff: he loves children, though, frequently beaten by his father, Mad Dog is determined not to bring a kid of his own into this vale of tears. "Aw come on," he said to the three-year-old, "what's your name?" The child blinked several times. Sniffled, looked around. Shifted in Mad Dog's arms, pulled away from the sweat-soaked Boston Celtics T-shirt. And then, fixing his eyes on Mad Dog's, his voice very small and quite tremulous, the child said, "My name is Anwar Sadat."

But all this happened the summer before, the writer's previous trip back to Boston. And anyway, to do justice to the day he and Mad Dog played ball down by the Charles, one would have to note that the court is on the corner of Flagg Street, which puts it only a block from the apartment the writer and two roommates rented their last year of college. That would be 1964–65. The manager, a person of large ambitions and commensurate failures, lived right downstairs. Once, he drastically receded his hairline and obliterated his eyebrows in the act of relighting a hot water heater's pilot. And sometimes he'd beat his wife. "Hitting me won't give you an erection," she'd scream. Listening very carefully, the writer thought this was real life, was very glad they'd moved off campus.

But the summer we're speaking of, several summers ago, the writer was back in Boston having just finished his novel and in need of a rest. In need of therapy, really: how to come back into the wide world. It seemed like years since he'd really gone somewhere. Friends would leave for a walking trip to Peru, a sail in the Adriatic. "I'm going to El Cerrito next week," the writer would tell them. El Cerrito being the next town north. Some joke. But for quite a while it was in fact about as far as he got, and, truth be told, he wouldn't have accepted a free ticket to Bali. Everything not in his novel simply too sheer to be real.

Done with it, finally, he concluded he was exhausted not

just from writing but from his thirty-nine years on the planet. Worse, he diagnosed in himself a kind of agoraphobia. He thought of a friend who, intrepid when young, became unable to venture out of the house alone after the death of her father. Amazingly, still she managed to finish law school, marry twice, work, and have a child. Her example, unfortunately, gave the writer no cheer. His agoraphobia would be different. To begin with, no one would come by to help. Clearly, he had to get himself moving.

Once in Boston, after several days the writer proceeded north to Maine. The family of an old friend's wife had a place on the coast. Several years before he'd attended their wedding in Virginia. Dinner on the eve of the ceremony in a hunt club, fox heads on plaques on the wall. Honkies, and not afraid to say so! If marriage suggests a struggle to see which of two families will reproduce, then this appeared a classic in the making, old money versus immigrant esthetes. Consider the toast given by the groom's father: "To my oldest son: Poet." You could hear the eyeballs rolling.

Everyone was drunk by then, younger set waiting for the fossils to leave so they could skinnydip in the club pool. A woman of perhaps thirty sat at the writer's table. About to be ordained a minister, she informed him. Previous experience with *est*. And what did he think about the wedding? Which led to some opinions concerning the role of the church in modern American life and her conclusion: the church is the only remaining source of moral guidance.

"Now hold it right there," the writer said. "I don't know as how I could agree with that." Three thousand miles from California, having just jetted across the Sierra, Rockies, and the great heartland, he felt simple, agrarian, next to these Eastern sophisticates. "No, ma'am," he said. "For one thing, I don't believe you can tell a story without takin' sides. Without a point of view, if you see what I mean."

The next day, hundreds of guests in attendance, Clydesdales hauling wagonloads of children, a drunk and very buxom woman at the reception began to unbutton the writer's black silk shirt to "see whose breasts are bigger." Her fingers about down to his sternum when, into the far right corner of his peripheral vision, came massive shoulders and arms that could only belong to her husband.

So it was the summer home of his friend's wife's family to which the writer consigned himself after the novel to cure his agoraphobia. He'd been to the Maine coast as a child, thirty years before. Returning, he seemed in some kind of time warp. Shingles still weathered just so. The leisure strenuous, followed by tea and popovers. Everyone in garish plaid Bermuda shorts, obviously some kind of birth control.

The first evening, stomachs full of lobster and linguine, he and his old friend sat on small chaises looking out at the fjord, the writer thinking of 1965, when he and his friend had shared an apartment. "He's Hercules, I'm Samson," his friend had told the neighborhood kids when they moved in. The kids would come looking for the writer. "Where's Herc?" they'd ask.

The next night, after a day of sailing, they attended a post-regatta dinner. Host an investment banker in New York City. Wife in her late thirties, slight east-European accent. Her second marriage, his third. New baby girl. He flew up weekends, "four hundred plus / plus / per." At one point, dinner finished, the wife poured the writer a cup of coffee in the kitchen. "So what do you write about?" she asked.

"Oh, lately it's been men and women in and out of love. Death. Growing up. Family. That kind of thing."

Surveying the living room, where her husband was issuing cigars to the men, she nodded thoughtfully. "You know," she said, "there are two kinds of souls." She paused. "Old souls and new souls." She stared out at her husband. "New souls are often quite crude."

Later that evening the husband sat down beside him. "They say you're a writer."

"Yes."

"So what's it like? Is it hard?"

"Well, to tell you the truth, sometimes it reminds me of a thing I saw when I was nineteen. In Copenhagen, a place called Tivoli."

"I've been there. The amusement park."

"Right. Anyway, in one of the acts, a man began with a handstand, then stood on one hand. Then on one finger. Finally, he went up a flight of stairs like that. Hop, hop, hop. And that was it. I guess my point is, sometimes writing makes me think of that man. Doing something difficult, something kind of absurd, and there's probably at least a small audience watching."

The investment banker puffed on his cigar, sipped his drink. "You know," he finally said, "I don't believe it."

"What in particular is it that you don't believe?" the writer asked.

"I don't know," the banker replied. "I guess I just don't believe a man can climb a flight of stairs on one finger."

*T*HEY say that for each person there are two stories: the life one intended, and the life one led.

No doubt savoring the verb, Joan Didion said, "Writers are always selling somebody out." Though she should perhaps have eschewed generalization in favor of confession, it is true that some people are leery of writers. For good reason, according to Strindberg. "What an occupation," he wrote. "To sit and flay your fellow men and then offer their skins for sale and expect them to buy them. To be like a hunter, who in need chops off his dog's tail, and after eating the flesh himself, offers the dog his bones, his own bones." Which brings to mind the Greek word *allelophago*, from *allelos*, one another, and *phago*, from *phagein*, to eat. For the ancients the point might have been that while fish and birds consume their own kind, humans should not.

Years ago, just after the writer's first book was published, a friend asked that the writer never make him a character. (This reference aside, it should be noted, the writer never has.) Another friend, otherwise voluble, pointedly never spoke to the writer about her divorce, although several members of their circle were privy to every grisly detail. On the other hand, there's the couple who tell people that one of his stories is "about us," as if he'd taken a photograph, perhaps.

Then there's the woman the writer briefly dated years ago. Occasionally, still, he sees her at the nearby schoolyard, where they both run a few miles on the track at sunset. "It's not just that I don't want you to write anything people think is me," she once told the writer. "It's that *I* don't want to read it and think it's me. Understand?" He did, he did, but then one day as they circled the field, hundreds of kids chasing soccer balls, coaches screaming out orders, parents on the sidelines, joggers thick as rush-hour traffic, the emotionally needy running against the grain, she told the writer that her husband had become "very paranoid." Clues to the massive nationwide conspiracy he'd unearthed were there to be deciphered by any truly careful reader of the work of two well-known columnists in the daily *San Francisco Chronicle*. She didn't really believe it, she said, but had decided to go along "for a few years." She laughed. "You never know. Maybe he's right." Though she laughed again, suddenly she seemed uneasy. Not, perhaps, because she felt she'd betrayed her husband by confiding in the writer, but because of course the conspiracy was very powerful. Someone might be listening. One of the joggers, maybe. One of the coaches.

The writer was sick at heart. What to say? What to do? Was there some normal life to which she could be restored? Were there deprogrammers who could kidnap a wife from the cult of her husband? "I know this sounds foolish," he finally responded, "but if we were all twenty years younger I'd call your parents."

She laughed. "Oh, you don't have to worry. Really. I'm OK." Abruptly, she looked back over her shoulder. "Just don't tell anyone, all right?"

"All right. All right."

"Promise?"

"I promise," the writer said.

W__RITING__ in *Adam's Task* about language, communication between animals and human beings, and *virtu*, Vicki Hearne argues that champion equestrian Hans Winkler was able to ride the intense and sensitive mare Halla to a Grand Prix in part "because he had a better story to tell himself and her about the nature of horsemanship and horses than riders who failed with her did. . . . He had to have had, for one thing, a story about how what appears to be horse insanity may be—even must be, most of the time—evidence of how powerful equine genius is, and how powerfully it can object to incoherence."

As it happened, in the penultimate round of the Grand Prix, equestrian Winkler pulled a groin muscle, was in the final round unable to use his legs—therefore essentially without a way to control Halla. Nonetheless, they negotiated the dangerous course to victory. For Hearne, "Riders who have a lot of stories about incurably crazy horses tend to find that a lot of the horses they run into are incurably crazy. The stories we tell matter. . . ."

LISTS. The writer keeps a list of things to do, retypes it most mornings. His friend Scott once caught him at this. Certain he'd beheld the naked face of compulsion, Scott waited for an auspicious moment to add a final item: Breathe in.

Whenever the writer prepares to travel he compiles a second list. For instance:

typewriter(?)

high-tops

razor

And so on. Functional, this list, but also, typed on his old Selectric, a bridge between smaller and larger worlds. For the writer, leaving home has come to be synonymous with leaving writing behind. Whatever its virtues, the larger world is too sheer, too imminent for writing. More, out in it he is someone else. A person who has written, who will no doubt write again.

"You writers are lucky," someone once tells him. "You can work anywhere." Thinking perhaps of Hemingway, Maugham, London, Stevenson (though who knows, maybe even they wrote only at home). The writer ponders the matter. Of course he can relocate; surely he's more mobile than a physician or lawyer with a practice. But it is also true that to write he needs the continuities of a steady life, a de facto commitment to one perspective, cultivation of one self in one place. From which emerges voice, vision. Writing, it seems, is in part a function of a willingness to say, "This is where I draw the line, no matter what I could learn or could be elsewhere, even if I could or should have moved on."

Once, the night before the writer is to start a trip, his friend Bill comes in to the cottage, sees he's accumulated enough gear on the living room rug to outfit a safari. "The point of travel is to leave it all behind," Bill says, no doubt envisioning a pack on the writer's back. The writer surveys the heap. Could be worse, actually: the accumulation is no more than the very least he needs at this in-between moment—being already gone but somehow still here—to maintain a connection to his life as a writer. Copy of each of his books. File folders with notes for projects. List of story ideas. Photos of friends, cottage. Photos of the bookshelves (lighter than carrying the books). Barely enough: already he misses the car. He considers freeze-drying, adding water to a vial of silver nuggets when he reaches his destination. *Voilà!* His '78 Camaro.

That night the cat dozes on one of the writer's bags. Comprehending the obvious, she knows he's going. He tries to imagine what she'll see while he's away. Her normal round. Out the cat door in the morning to the roof of the studio. Nap on skylight. Garden in afternoon. Possum. Doves, bees, ants, squirrels. The iris. The raccoon family. Siamese from down the block. Mailman, garbage truck, UPS. Sun. Shadow. Wind. Crane flies on bathroom wall. Fog. Night. Neighbor coming over to spoon out catfood.

The neighbor. As usual, the writer leaves her a note. Typed, of course. Where he'll be, when. Phone numbers. Schedule. An argument of sorts—I SHALL RETURN. Washing the dishes, putting things away one more once, making eye contact with the cat, the writer knows that this—the small, the quotidian—is what is true.

In the morning he closes the door to his study, locks it. Checks to be sure the cat is not shut in. And then, *poof,* a writer no more, he heads out through first one and then another gate, lugging two incredibly heavy bags. Off 3,000 miles to Boston, New York, Washington. Voyageur. Explorer. Conquistador. Wondering if he'll be back. If he'll be himself when he gets back. If he'll find the part of himself that will need to, will be able to, tell the story.

⌒ ⌒ ⌒

"Collect from Jack in Buffalo," the operator says. "Will you accept the charges?"

"Where?" the writer asks.

"Buffalo."

"All right."

"Go ahead please."

"Jack."

"Hey, man, I'm stranded. They threw me off the bus. You got to wire me a hundred so I can get home."

"Jesus, Jack, right now I don't have it. Can't you ask somebody else?"

"Hey, there is no one else. I kid you not."

The writer had last heard from Jack several months before, a call—not collect—from his mother's place in San Diego.

"How is it, Jack?"

"Slow man, slow."

"You going to stay?"

"What do you think? Should I stay? How's Frisco?"

"I really don't know what to tell you. Seems pretty tough these days."

"I could try Mexico. You think Mexico, man?"

The writer knew Jack from Cambridge. Back in town for a visit, he'd wander around Harvard Square, bump into Jack again. There'd be a Bogart film at the Brattle and they'd sit on the steps, breeze coming off the river, rain threatening. Jack chain smoking, popping multivitamins. "Hey, man, check that one out," Jack would exclaim, though he'd said that vitamins made him impotent.

For years Jack did the rounds looking to score. Cafe Pamplona. Blue Parrot. Casablanca. Harvard Bookstore. Wordsmith. Reading International. Up Bow Street, down Mass Ave, across Boylston, along Mount Auburn.

"Hey, man, I'm screwed up, I haven't written anything lately."

Not for years, actually, and not even during the years he was a "writer" picking up women in the Square, always some Pynchon or Gaddis and a notebook under his arm. God, it was a fantastic rap for a while, but then Jack began to wonder. Was he a writer? Well—no. A reader, really, he loved books, but the girls would never have gone for that, would they?

"*I REALLY* liked your stories," the woman told the writer. "They made me think of one you could use in your next book. Want to hear it?"

"Sure."

"Well, about five years ago my husband and I were fighting all the time. About everything. You name it, we fought about it. Among other things we fought about was the temperature in the bedroom at night. Particularly in winter. Whether to leave the window open for some fresh air, how many blankets, that kind of issue. You can just imagine. Then one day I was out shopping in Chestnut Hill and I saw a thermal blanket with two separate control dials, a dial for each side of the blanket. This could save the marriage, I said to myself. I bought it right away, told them not to bother with a box. As soon as I got home I put it on our bed. God, I was high as a kite. You probably don't believe me."

"No, no, I do. Really. Please go on."

"Well, the strange thing was, the new thermal blanket didn't help a bit. I was still always too hot at night, sweltering, sweating, suffocating, while my husband was forever complaining about freezing to death. Same old song. Spring came. We decided to separate. It was only the next winter, sleeping alone under the thermal blanket, that I suddenly realized . . ."

". . . that he'd been using your dial and you'd been using his."

"That's it," she said, grinning. "That's the story."

P‍ART of being a writer is the capacity to live with imperfection, particularly as a work of fiction first takes shape. Not that this is always easy for any artist. Consider Mary McCarthy's story about Michelangelo, who in his old age became dissatisfied with a Pietà he intended for his own tomb. "Instead of simply abandoning work on it, as he had done with so many of his commissions, this time he took a hammer and began to smash it to pieces." Apparently, this Pietà has since been restored: "one of the dead Christ's nipples has been mended, but His left arm is still badly scarred by the hammer blows. The figure of Nicodemus, an old man in a cowl who is supposed to represent Michelangelo, is barely sketched into the stone."

This kind of testimony notwithstanding, and no matter how the writer protests, people generally assume that art is cathartic for the artist. Further, appraising fiction as autobiographical in some simple sense, they're certain that to write a story frees the writer of its content. Sometimes he counters that of course language and form mediate between even "fact" and what reaches the page. That fiction and the process of writing it are new events, whatever the point of departure. Or, he asks, what if writing is like method acting? Take on a role, reach for the analogous part of the self. Is to play Lear or Oedipus to feel better? Or, as Caudwell suggests, are poetic creations simply the vehicle of neurosis, still one more disguise? All these arguments, however, do little to deflect the genial extension of Aristotle's thesis about the effect of tragedy on the spectator. Art's cathartic, don't you see?

Back in 1976, nearing the end of a book of stories and thinking it a stern vision he'd conjured, the writer emerged from the movies one night to find a ticket on his windshield. "You dirty bastards," he muttered: twenty-four-hour meters. Unlocking the car door, he took out the tire iron, people streaming past toward their vehicles. Swinging very smoothly, taking it easy at first so as not to pull a muscle, he began to clobber the meter. Finally, a crowd around him, the writer administered a death blow, meter expiring with an exhalation of nickels and dimes. "Enough," he said, mostly to himself, and then drove off.

There's also the time he was working on the final draft of his novel. He'd drive over to the Y several days a week to play basketball. It was only eight or nine blocks, but always he'd drive. That particular afternoon, an aging freak in a battered AMC Pacer cut him off. And then, a minute or two later, cut him off again. The writer was wild; the freak just had to know he was doing it. The second time, the writer smiled to himself to think of making a citizen's arrest. Now that would blow the so-and-so's mind.

A block later he pulled up behind the Pacer at a red light. He subsequently remembered seeing his hand on the emergency brake. He also remembered thinking it might be great to bash in the Pacer's taillights, but as he slammed the door behind him he realized he hadn't taken the tire iron. So where was he going? And then he found himself motioning to the freak to roll down his window. It should be added that the writer was wearing white Nike high-tops, sweat pants, hooded Harvard sweatshirt, down vest, and black beret.

"I'm just finishing my shift," the writer heard himself shout, "and I'm tired as hell. But if you want me to write you up, I'll write you up. Cutting me off twice, you must want it real bad."

"I'm sorry, officer," the freak began, but then, light having changed, the car behind the writer's started to honk. "Pull up over there," the writer said, pointing to the curb on the far side of the intersection, turning to glower at the people who'd honked. Couldn't they see this was official business? Getting in behind the wheel, he came alongside the Pacer, driver now standing there waiting. The writer glared at him, then impatiently waved as if to say he was too small a fish and was being thrown back in. Stepping on the gas, the writer pulled around the corner, parked, and waited for his aorta to stop howling.

Now. Swinging the tire iron at the meter, that was cathartic. And impersonating a police officer, well, you can see how this might eliminate bile. But writing? *Writing?* For the love of God, it was writing that was making him crazy. Of course, if one stops to think it over, those were smooth strokes with the tire iron, and in dealing with the guy in the Pacer there was a sort of method in the writer's madness. Hell, maybe even some kind of art involved.

A MONTH after they started seeing each other, they were in each other's arms one night, had just made love.

"Tell me what I looked like," she said.
"When?"
"The night we met."
"The night we met? How you looked?"
"Yes."
"You looked good."
"No."
"You did. Very good."
"No."
"No what?"
"Tell me what it was like when you saw me."
"What it was like?"
"Yes."
"When?"
"Then. That night."
"The night I saw you?"
"Yes."
"Please?"
"Please."
"Please what?"
"Please tell me."
"Tell you what?"
"The story."
"What story?"
"The story of the night we met."

*I*T was in fourth grade that the writer first used the word frugal in classroom discussion. Perhaps both word and context stay with him because at age eight he might better have described himself as profligate. For instance, on the upstairs hall table was a small wooden bowl from Mexico in which his father would deposit excess coins. Often the writer would raid the bowl, take out his Schwinn, and head for Irving's Variety Store to buy nonpareils or several boxes of Good and Plenty (pink or white sugar-coated licorice, which were, as the ad said, Plenty Good). Not that the children couldn't take money from the bowl, yet clearly there was a limit. Which, more than once, the writer exceeded.

But the words: frugal profligate. Ordinary enough to him by eight or nine, part of the family vernacular. Coming home from school, he'd walk in the back door, perhaps to find his mother upstairs surveying the park, pond, and willows, again writing about this view. Or she'd be reading: Emily Dickinson, Gilbert White, Henri Fabre. Or she'd be standing in front of the wall mirrors rehearsing, say, Edith Sitwell's *Façade* for an upcoming concert.

> SAILORS come
> To the drum
> Out of Babylon;
>    Hobby-horses
> Foam, the dumb
> Sky rhinosceros-glum

> Or:
> So do not take a bath in Jordan, Gordon,
> On the holy Sabbath on the peaceful day—
> Or you'll never go to heaven, Gordon Macpherson,
> And speaking purely as a private person

> That is the place—*that* is the place—that is the
> *place* for me.

The words and music of *Façade* permeated a year or two of the writer's childhood, became part of the household vocabulary. Yet even then his mother was moving away from her career as a celebrated performer of lieder and art songs: in 1954, her first volume of poems was published. The four children joked that their father had bought the entire printing; there were cases and cases out in the porch room.

Though the writer's mother had once studied philosophy, she seemed to abhor generalization; the specific, closely—ferociously—observed, was what redeemed. Gerard Manley Hopkins her guide, she wrote poems like this:

> *Sometimes the Soul*
> Sometimes the soul
> so quiet stays in seas
> of self, as cedars still-
> standing in breathless space,
>
> as though the truce
> of trees grew calm in clear
> compress of crystal vise:
> fossil within the air.
>
> No shrug of leaf,
> no animus exhumes
> axis, aura, and stiff
> uncommingling limbs,
>
> not till the draft of hand or wind infer
> a to and fro, a lift,
> a lulling as before.

And, later, this:

> Under the cherry bough,
> fallen May-bloom lies
> prone: slow-melting snow.

One petal-pair alone
has drifted off the heaped
spring blench toward June.

Two flakes hurtle twinned
across wide sun, finding
wild plants to feed their daring.

Mustard, cabbage, sleep.
Meadows away from where
burst the terse bud,

the matched halves of moth
settle as with one need,
face down and cheek to earth.

O love, my other wing.

    For the writer's mother, art was not simply to please but to instruct. "Opportunities" of the kind her children received entailed "responsibilities." To this end, language was the primary mode of socialization (to use just the kind of jargon she loathed). Oh, on rare occasions the writer's father took his belt out, but "haywire," "selfish," "bickering," "snotty," these were words that could control. And wound. "Poopsie," for instance: stop feeling sorry for yourself.

    The four children, raucous at dinner, teased that their father couldn't understand her poems. Of course he could, though her early bravura verse conceded little to any reader, but they also knew that for pleasure he read mysteries. His real rapport with his wife's commitment to the arts came at the end of her concerts, when he'd be first on his feet with a basso BRAVA, BRAVA, embarrassing and pleasing the rest of the family claque.

    He also loved wordplay. Committing a pun a dinner, saying "excuse me" as he laughed. Or pointing out that it had to be an initial long "i" in annihilation because the Pharoah would have been crossing the—Nile. In addition, he gave his children *"Psia krew dupa swinia paskudny . . . ,"* a string of Polish curses and imprecations (dog's blood, etc.). They never heard him swear in English, and the Polish, so theatrically un-American, deflated anger even before the words were out. Not understanding the Polish, one of the children would spill some milk, mutter *"Psia krew. . . ."* "Don't say that," he'd warn, tears of laughter in his eyes.

He published the first of several hundred scientific papers in his early twenties, wrote a text on autopsy technique soon after. "The heart is grasped at the apex by the left hand and drawn upward and forward. The great vessels are then severed by horizontal knife strokes."

And: "The following slight refinement in technique has proved of value. After the external examination of the body has been made, the face of the patient is covered with a towel secured behind the head by a clamp or towel clip. Similarly, a towel is placed across the legs, over the genitalia. This procedure takes but a moment and adds dignity to the examination."

Perhaps his single most important paper was "Temporary Remissions in Acute Leukemia in Children Produced by Folic Acid Antagonist 4-Aminopteryl-Glutamic Acid (Aminopterin):" "Clinical, hematologic, and histological details of 5 patients with acute leukemia treated with Aminopterin, selected from a group of 16 patients so treated, form the basis of this paper. . . . It is again emphasized that these remissions are temporary in character and that the substance is toxic. . . . No evidence has been mentioned in this report that would justify the suggestion of the term 'cure' of acute leukemia."

Such cautious language. He had just created the field of chemotherapy in cancer, would soon build a hospital for the care of cancer in children. This was a revolution, and in so prudently reporting his findings, he braced for hostile reaction from those who knew cancer to be monolithic and beyond remedy. Further, in speeches, papers, and testimony before Congress, he called for "total care" of the patient and the patient's family and for massive government support for medical research. "May I urge you to regard as intolerable the delay between discovery in the laboratory or clinic and application to the patient?" he asked. "May I urge, too, that you join forces in breaking down the artificial barriers between departments, between institutions, between workers, during this vital period of medical research which must and will lead to the solution of so many problems responsible today for suffering, and disease, and death?"

The public voice of the writer's father, not entirely unlike his voice at home. The children knew he'd been ill and still struggled with his health. They knew he cared for dying children. They knew he was famous—people stopped them on the street to thank him through them—though they never heard about the countless awards from either parent. But even as presidents and senators found irresistible his appeal that they fund research and service to children in need, so the four children at home understood that all he hoped for from them was "whatever you really want." And just how did this translate? Well, there was the little verse he sometimes recited, always looking a bit bemused, never offering it as more than an odd remnant of his childhood. "Good / better / best, never let it rest, till the good is better and the better is best."

The language of the household. It could almost have been a libretto: someone was always practicing, rehearsing, off to class, concert, recital. Piano, for all the children, at Mrs. Keaney's, across from the high school football team's practice field. Then a second instrument. The writer's was cello, which he hated. He'd close the sliding French doors to the music room, wait as a half-hour elapsed. How slowly he could unpack the cello, how many times he would rosin the bow. With the trumpet, however, he found an extraordinary teacher, by high school was playing with a brass group in churches. Gabrielli, Purcell, Bach. Once, running late on a snowy winter morning because he'd overslept after a date, the group arrived at the church to find the congregation praying for its safety.

The music of the home. When the writer's younger sister left for college the house was sold, the pianos given away. Long since, their mother had given her full energies to verse. Now what she knew about music would be found only there. For years the writer could make little of her poetry. Formal, intricate, full of allusions, it eluded him. Was too arch, ironic, sublimated, demanding. Yet at twenty-three, suddenly he was beginning to write, would soon speak of the "melodies" of the lives he'd encountered in California in the sixties. Struggling to escape a world of too many responsibilities, he'd gone too far. But then, fancying himself a kind of singer of songs, in desperate need of order and work and a way to reconcile all he'd experienced, he found a voice. Writing, writing, he both celebrated and measured the lives he'd encountered three thousand miles from home, doing so in the tongue of the life he'd left behind. He wanted the book to be their—his—memoir, apologia. Words would have the power to dignify, justify, save.

This language, these tones. Songs his mother and father taught him. Songs of the home they built and sustained. As his mother wrote, "If the bread I broke with the world was music, the cup I shared was words."

NABOKOV said a writer can be considered a storyteller, teacher, or enchanter, a real writer being "the fellow who sends the planets spinning and models a man asleep and eagerly tampers with the sleeper's rib. . . ." In a somewhat similar vein, Thoreau gives us his fable of the artist of Kouroo, whose "singleness of purpose and resolution, and his elevated piety, endowed him, without his knowledge, with perennial youth." Before he'd even chosen the right materials for his staff his friends had all died. "By the time he had smoothed and polished it Kalpa was no longer the polestar, and ere he had put on the ferule and the head adorned with precious stones, Brahma had awoke and slumbered many times." Finally, as the staff was at last completed, "it suddenly expanded before the eyes of the astonished artist into the fairest of all the creations of Brahma. He had made a new system in making a staff, a world with full and fair proportions. . . . The material was pure, and his art was pure, how could the result be other than wonderful?"

His own perspective not quite so breathless, John Updike describes the writer as a reader moved to emulation, the artistic impulse as a mix "of childhood habits of fantasizing brought on by not necessarily unhappy periods of solitude; a certain hard wish to perpetuate and propagate the self; a craftsmanly affection for material and process; a perhaps superstitious receptivity to moods of wonder; and a not-mentioned-enough ability, within the microcosm of the art, to organize, predict and persevere."

While Updike's appraisal is clearly more down-to-earth than Thoreau's or Nabokov's, the highminded acumen of the prose itself nonetheless elevates the writer. More recently, however, playing with the notion that "the creative imagination wants to please its audience" by "sharing what is most precious to it," Updike invokes Freud's idea that the "child's first gift, presented to its parents, are its feces." Just as in this "primal benefaction," Updike ventures, "the writer extrudes his daily product while sitting down, on a healthy basis of regularity and avoidance of strain," sharing with the reader "nothing less than his digested life."

Oh well: the artist now playing not enchanter but early adolescent. A pose that could lead us toward Howard Nemerov's notion of the writer as perhaps no more than "the weak criminal whose confession implicates the others."

*THE* craft of writing. As many writers have complained, early drafts seem the most difficult. Both plot and language articulating it are being discovered simultaneously. Each step forward appears to imply revision of what has come before, and to abide so much that is raw requires patience, trust.

With subsequent drafts, dreaming of the story increasingly achieved, the latent ever more explicit, this process becomes more palpably physical. The hunger here is for compression. To eliminate repetition, to identify the inadvertent: "to flense," to strip blubber or skin from a whale or seal; "to winch down," tightening a sail to avoid slippage, drift. Finally, there is a sense of the story as clay on the potter's wheel. The writer, hands on, shaping, smoothing.

"It's between him and myself," the man tells the writer. Zen and the art of grammar. Though the writer read voraciously in what was then called grammar school, he couldn't quite master the mechanics of language, was never at ease when he had to diagram what Ezra Pound described as "that which acts and that which is acted upon, directly or indirectly, or that which is just standing around. . . ." Understanding began only with the declension of nouns in Latin class in high school, seeing in this inflected language different endings of the word as use varied. Nominative, genitive, dative, accusative, ablative. *Femina, feminae, feminae, feminam, femina.* The woman, of the woman, to the woman, for the woman, by the woman. For years, the writer had been sent to the dictionary whenever a word was in question, the Latin root often giving a kind of freedom by revealing the word's origin and so its vector. Now, studying Latin, finally beginning to understand its structure, he felt a new power, gratitude.

Punctuation he was already at peace with thanks to Danish comedian-pianist Victor Borge. In one routine, Borge assigned each mark of punctuation a sound (blat, gurgle, grunt, beep, chirp) and then recited a hackneyed text, something like "Under the spreading chestnut tree . . . ," punctuating it with the appropriate sounds. As the writer laughed, it dawned on him that written language was like written music (which long since he could read, sight-read). Each was a system of notation. If so, then perhaps commas, periods, semicolons, parentheses, and dashes possessed duration, pitch, volume. It also occurred to him that language, being sound, could be considered a kind of music.

"It's between him and myself," the man has just said to the writer. Could have been worse—"It's between he and myself." In this case, however, the man probably refrained from "It's between him and I." Against the better judgment of his ear, modesty's prevailed.

WHEN the woman the writer had lived with for eight years moved east to New York City, she left her cat. Not as a hostage, but because the cat had a good thing going in and around the cottage—its own small door (through which raccoon and possum occasionally made their way) and a semi-feral life, better than an apartment *mit* fire escape. Thus it was that the cat, seventeen, and the writer, forty-one, were seen one rainy morning heading down the street, cat in cardboard box, howling, moaning, and writer, carrying the box, consoling, cursing. An infected abscess on her shoulder, the cat was being transported to the vet's.

After surgery the cat recovered quickly, was soon well enough to race up the steep stairs to the loft, and, with apparent intent, to spill the writer's manuscript off the bureau. The writer, on the other hand, recovered rather more slowly, not entirely enchanted with the sight of her stitches or shaved shoulder, traumatized by the twice-daily battle to get pills down her throat, encounters during which they fought like—well, you know.

Even after so many years, the writer could hardly say he liked or disliked cats. It was more that he knew this particular animal. To begin with, he worked at home, saw few humans during the day. He'd go out in the yard to sit in the sun and the cat would materialize—from where?—to join him, calling as she came around the corner of the fence, always plopping over on her side just beyond arm's length.

Perhaps another bond between them was that both were curious. The writer, cat so familiar yet still exotic, had the need to understand her world. A writer should write about what he knows? Reasonable enough. Yet the writer could learn what he knew only by finding the words. Short of that, he still knew something: something else, something less. Of a cat character inspired by this living animal, the writer discovered that "old, black, and savvy," she had a way of jumping into her mistress's lap "following not the shortest trajectory, the hypotenuse of the right triangle formed by destination, floor directly beneath it, and point of departure—but sailing up, around, and over in a rich arc that carried her well above . . . before, as if rediscovering gravity, she dropped straight down on it, landing light as a feather and without a sound. Without a sound, that is, until she responded to being petted, her purr crackling like a two-cycle chain-saw running at idle."

Writing this, he experienced great pleasure, something like what Adam, recent arrival in God's world, must have felt to name the creatures in it ("And out of the ground the Lord God formed every / beast of the field, and every fowl of the air; and / brought *them* unto Adam to see what he would call them . . ."). The pleasure of naming. Of the same cat character the writer had written that, watching her mistress play with a toy mouse, she approaches, gives a "plaintive What-do-I-do-with-this? call, and suddenly begins batting it back and forth, rolling from side to side, teasing the poor thing almost to life before—whack!—administering the coup de grâce. Then, as abruptly as she began [she] sits back on her haunches, stares abstractedly at some dust in the corner."

If, writing this, the writer felt like Adam, he also felt a bit like God. Composer Ned Rorem said nothing exists "unless it is notated, not even the smell of the wind." Did the writer concur, was he some kind of closet (Bishop) Berkeleyan? Well . . . no. If pushed, he would concede the cat her own life. And concede that others could see a cat there too. But what cat? Or, how much of what cat? Did they see a cat who snarled "simply because the opportunity presented itself, or perhaps to keep her mind off other things?" No, they did not. And though they too heard a purr, that purr, even, did it "crackle" for them? Not without the writer, it didn't.

One night, this particular cat, to whatever degree one perceived it, hunched on the foot of the writer's bed, on the edge of the quilt with giraffe motif her mistress had made. Over the years writer and cat had worked out sleeping arrangements, writer not pleased to have her on the bed at all, cat loath not to sleep on the writer's chest. From the distance of six feet or so, then, pupils dilating, she was staring at him, neither of them completely content. The writer had put in a good day at his desk, was ready for sleep. "Think about this," he said to the cat. *"J'écris, donc je suis.* I write, therefore I am. Get the reference?" The cat began to purr—like a two-cycle chain-saw running at idle, so to speak. *"J'écris, donc tu es,"* the writer then said. "I write, therefore you are. Understand?" The cat closed her eyes.

Turning out the light, the writer saw the shape of the cat at the foot of the bed, hoped she wouldn't try to move up during the night. As he dozed off, the image of her hunched there evoked a word. "Egyptian," he said to himself, hoping to remember it in the morning, too tired to get up and write it down. "Scarabs," he heard himself mutter, and tried for a moment to picture his high school girlfriend and her scarab bracelet, the effort to recall the connection of scarabs, beetles, and Pharaohs blocked by an image of his girlfriend's mother. "A sarcophagus cat." Though suddenly he could see the phrase ruby-red on the screen of his inner eye, in that same instant he found himself utterly beyond any impulse to discover whatever it was the words might have to say.

An early-winter dinner party in Paris, before and through the meal and then with coffee everyone chainsmoking, lighting up again, talking nonstop with the ebullience of people in love with the sheer sound of their own voices. Over by the television, an expatriate English recording engineer in his mid-thirties, eight years now in France, gives the writer vicious sketches of the various guests—this would-be pederast, the director; that bankrupt adulterer, the producer—at a decibel level that is surely too high, using English as though it renders him invisible. Several times he winks at the writer as he concludes a libel, as if to say that the words of a well-turned phrase warrant both the risk of hyperbole and whatever suffering might have occasioned them. Periodically one of the other guests approaches, says hello, asks the Englishman where Suzanne is. Oh, she's away, they've been calling each other and missing, she's been traveling, he himself's been wondering when she'll get back, etc. etc. After hearing several such exchanges, the writer idly hazards to himself that the Englishman and the absent Suzanne have known each other—lived with each other? lived with each other on and off?—for some years, since before they both came—together?—to Paris.

Finally, after the Englishman says something about Suzanne's wonderful apartment in the Marais, the writer bites: "What does Suzanne do?"

The Englishman smiles. "Oh, Suzanne? She's a call girl here in Paris and has a sugar daddy in Rome."

SOME visitors find the cottage too spare. It should be said, however, that in the writer's study there are several large bookcases teeming with books. As the writer construes it, all of them were written by human beings. Sometimes, sitting at his desk, he turns around and sees a homunculus standing in front of each binding. Shelves lined with homunculi, desperate homunculi beating their breasts, screaming, "Read me, read me!"

At least two hundred books in his study, not to mention the manuscript he's working on, the writer tries to keep the rest of the cottage as bare as he can.

◁ ◁ ◁

"I HATE to say it," the old man tells the writer though there's no stopping him. "I hate to say it, but before you know it there'll be a nigger president in the White House." The old man is Greek, and they're in the Aegean, chugging east from Athens toward the Cyclades. He's heading home after thirty years of restaurant work in Manhattan. Approaching thirty, the writer is heading away from home. One book out, another in mind, he's grown allergic to invective, vituperation. It's mid-1972, and in English nearly every word is loaded. The endless war, the war at home. The writer wants to be somewhere he doesn't speak the language.

Stone walls. Donkey shit. Whitewash. Moon Tiger flypaper. King Kong mosquito coils. Bare light bulbs. Carillons of goat bells, the goatherd's whistles, the donkey's groans. Small green terraces, bare hillsides, blue sky, Homer's wine-dark sea. The Pleiades. Worry beads. Knock-knees, cross-eyes. Short-handled brooms. Stars coming out like sounds: *ping, ping.* Moonsets, the blinding glare of mid-day. She and the writer breaking up, though, finally forgiving the absence of hot water, she shows him the color wheel. White contains all colors, she explains. Black is no color at all.

*Kalimera. Yiasou. Ohi. Parakalo. Ne. Nero. Lahdi. Epharisto poli. Tikanis. Kala.* This is all the Greek the writer knows, and of course the script is unintelligible. Days, weeks, pass. He doesn't try to avoid learning more, but is content not to. He studies expressions, physiognomies, body language. Listens to words as sound. Is led, directed, shown, one of his guides a seven-year-old German boy. The writer can't speak German, but then neither can the boy, whose capacity for language seems limited to "Baba"—mother—and "Bubee"—me, myself. A wild child. Always he's tugging at the writer's hand, pointing, moaning, struggling for understanding. One day they're to go out fishing, boy standing by the dock wearing cowboy hat, mask, snorkel, fins. Just as the caïque arrives, however, suddenly he tears off the mask, pulls desperately at the writer's arm, begins to weep. His cheeks expand, then he blows out the air, shakes his head in desperation. Inhales again, exhales violently. Ah—wind. High wind. A storm. Palms joined, the boy moves a prow through the storm's dangerous seas, shows the boat going down.

Of course the writer doesn't go entirely without English. He thinks in English, talks to himself in English. Talks to her in English, though they seem to have little left to say. Mornings and afternoons are spent in silent proximity down on the rocks. She sketches, he dives. At night there is music in the cafes. Joe Cocker, the Beatles, the Stones, Joni Mitchell. "A Little Help from My Friends," "Yesterday," "Wild Horses," "Blue," the lyrics soon obliterated by the insistent Greek instrumentals, more eastern, more unsettling, than he could have imagined when he thought Greece part of Europe.

At night the writer bumps into Lady Jane, "Here to fuck the Greek men, darling." And Joe, so in need of housing that he propositions women with the line, "Do you want to go to bed?" And Jim, retired from the American army at forty, twenty and out, self-exiled to this island to stretch his pension. Sustaining himself with baseball on radio from US bases on Crete, with back issues of *Time* and the *Herald Tribune*, with retsina, and with his own idiom. "Christ, the fucker flattened the asshole." "See if the kid has any balls." "Here's champagne for our real friends and real pain for our sham friends." On the island four years now without a break, Jim speaks no Greek. "Why should I? They know where I'm coming from."

Running out of things to read, the writer learns that Jim has the only hoard of books on the island. Apparently he prefers mysteries, thrillers, and westerns, but saves everything against the interminable winters.

"Jim," the writer says one morning at the cafe. "Can I borrow some books?"

"Nope, No. N-o. Do I look like someone who loans books?"

"My mistake. How about if I bought some books from you?"

"Wrong again. Do I look like somebody who sells books?"

"Now that you mention it, I guess not," the writer replies, getting up to leave. "Thanks anyway."

"Just hold your horses. What's your rush? Don't you want to know what I do with books? Besides read 'em, that is?"

"All right, Jim. What do you do with books?"

"I trade 'em, that's what."

As it turns out, Jim trades by weight. "I don't give a flying fuck," he says. Scouting around the island, the writer comes up with *Bury My Heart at Wounded Knee, Soul on Ice,* and a Cheever, for which Jim gives him two Robert Graveses, a Conrad, and a Virginia Woolf.

Another month passes. The writer learns only a few more words of Greek, but has several visions, no doubt caused by reading Graves on Greek myths, or from swimming under the stars awash in phosphorescent plankton. She and the writer are at the end of their six-year dialogue, nearly beyond words, soon to leave but in no great rush. Nor is the writer hurrying to get home to listen to Gerald Ford explain why he had to pardon Nixon. To hear John Dean's "at that point in time" enter the vernacular. Or, taking the long road back to the US of A, to hear the Moroccan guide he does not hire say in *his* English: "You waste time, fucking hippy. You eat hash. You eat cock. You eat snake."

SOME writers imagine a kinship between themselves and the ancient bards, deprived if not of sight then of the capacity to function in the larger world. So becoming entitled, by way of compensation, to the gift of song. Too, they like to think they had no choice about what they became: writing called. As, perhaps, it does. But consider the case of Samuel Johnson. As a young man, Johnson was apparently interested in both schoolteaching and the law. According to Paul Fussell, he became a writer only "by default and by accident, prevented by poverty and ugliness from aspiring to any other life. He finally had to find a profession in which his shocking person could be concealed from his audience."

≺ ≺ ≺

M<small>IKEY</small> at three and three quarters. "A few days ago," he says for the first time: only recently has he been setting limits on the pure present. Rhyme also in the air: "scoop, scoop," he says, eyes twinkling, enjoying this alternative to the p-o-o-p word his mother felt she'd heard once too often. Her aversion triggered by the time—a few days ago, it was—he called her Dummypoop, surely then the strongest weapon in his verbal arsenal.

"I'm not going to be your friend." "The sunset is going down." "Please hold me." "You hurt my feelings." "I need a grownup to help." "Vagina." And, born out of discipline: "Thank you / not spank you."

Mikey and the monsters he likes to scare himself with—though only up to a point. Thus the tent monsters, off-season Santa Clauses who delivered his tent. And the shampoo monster, who administers his shampoos (and looks much like the writer, whose shirt the monster always steals just before lurching in the bathroom door). But of course monsters can be too real, a grownup needed in the middle of the night to drive out whatever's lurking in the closet.

Mikey's monsters, the nature of story: his creations, but occasionally beyond his control. Invented, but, like a writer's characters, finding a place in the actual world. And, perhaps, serving a preemptive or protective function: monsters, yes, but one's own and, possibly, the only ones there are.

*≤ ≤ ≤*

H<small>E</small> wrote his first stories about the dark side of love's moon while safe in the heart of their relationship. Confident in what they shared, he could stare without blinking at loneliness, betrayal, remorse, attenuation of desire.

However: increasingly possessed by the hunger to grasp his subject in all its qualities, he was capable of looking with a dispassionate eye on even what passed between them. That is, more than once, far from working to remedy a problem they encountered, he acted as though even the worst could teach him something he needed to learn.

FROM a United Press obituary of English poet Philip Larkin, we learn that "He spent his last 30 years as a university librarian in Hull, an unfashionable, decaying town suited to his retiring nature. . . . 'Deprivation is for me what daffodils were for Wordsworth,' he once said. . . . His meager output [four volumes in forty years] led him to decline last year the post of poet laureate. . . . Larkin shunned publicity and projected the gray aura of a dome-headed bachelor, usually wearing a drab suit."

The photo of Larkin accompanying this piece has the caption, "He dwelt on deprivation." Larkin is looking right at the camera, wearing glasses with heavy dark frames. Projecting, in fact, a rather gray aura. ("Actually," Larkin once said, "I like to think of myself as quite funny, and I hope this comes through in my writing. But it's unhappiness that provokes a poem. . . . As Montherlant says somewhere happiness writes white.") Regarding his childhood, an interviewer asked Larkin if it had really been as "unspent" as he suggested in one of his poems. "Oh," Larkin replied, "I've completely forgotten it."

Only half playing the curmudgeon, Larkin wasn't convinced poetry could be translated, that art should be subsidized, that poems should be read in performance. He felt he could have had a happier life only by being someone else, and that "it is very much easier to imagine happiness than to experience it." For him, the novel—he wrote two of them as a young man, would have liked to write more—was the richest literary form, could heighten our understanding of what we all must learn: "that nothing is absolute, that it is only we who are in love, or miserable, or about to die. . . ."

"I don't really notice where I live," Larkin once told a reporter. Not much. Consider his "This Be the Verse."

They fuck you up, your mum and dad.
    They may not mean to, but they do.
They fill you with the faults they had
    And add some extra, just for you.

But they were fucked up in their turn
    By fools in old-style hats and coats,
Who half the time were soppy-stern
    And half at one another's throats.

Man hands on misery to man.
    It deepens like a coastal shelf.
Get out as early as you can,
    And don't have any kids yourself.

EARLY January, sixty miles north of San Francisco. Slight shore breeze in across the fields. Shadows on brown hills, sun taking forever to set. Sheep tugging at grass. Docked lamb's tail near the foot of the cypress. Swallows pulsing in and out of the barn, singing, ratcheting.

Gate creaks. Falcon beats past. Air sweetens: the roses. Writer in the garden cutting a head of lettuce at the root, washing leaves under the tap, munching as ewes chew, stare.

Sunset, wind picking up. Ram coughs. Jupiter and Mars near the horizon to the south and west. Owl, screeching, wheeling down from the cypress, landing heavily on a lower branch.

Writer in the night, nowhere to go, waiting to see what's there, waiting to see what he'll see.

AGE seventy-four, three books forthcoming, the writer's mother has a stroke, is brought to the hospital.

*Deficiencies. Deficits. Areas of compromise.* She listens, weighs the possibility of metaphor. Her children—forty-five, forty-one, thirty-nine, and thirty-five—pass their visits reading to her. The mail. Gerard Manley Hopkins. Gilbert White's letters from Selborne. Emily Dickinson. French naturalist Henri Fabre. And her own poems. Her waist-length hair—still brown!—is braided, but, for the first time they can remember, not up and coiled. They give her chocolate. "Contraband," she calls it.

"How are you, Mother?" the writer asks.

"I thought in war they take the young."

*Life threatening. Risk of infection. ICU.* Vapor from the oxygen mask wells up, condensation collecting on her cheeks. Wires. Tubes. Needles. Bags. The writer tells his mother that his cab driver, an Ethiopian, didn't know the way in to Harvard Square from Logan Airport.

"But you did," she says.

"Yes."

"Good."

"So how is it?"

"If I begin to take this seriously, I'm lost."

His mother has toyed with a sequel to her *How Does It Feel To Be Old? How Does It Feel To Be Older?*, or *How Does It Feel To Be Posthumous?*. Now she suggests a book on stroke. A picture book, perhaps, for children.

"Random scan," the four children call it. Sometimes—due to the drugs, assault of the hospital regimen, or massive blows sustained—she spaces out. She's trying to remember something. At the foot of Beacon Hill. On Charles Street. First three letters B / O / N.

Another day, she says, "I'm diffused between centuries."

She also makes periodic references to going down to the Potomac. Her Potomac strategy, the children come to call it. An escape, perhaps, but why there? Black nurses, late night sounds of the hospital—whistles, bells, cries in the night. Is the hospital a steamboat? Or like Jack Kennedy's Washington: southern efficiency, northern charm.

Spaced out. Is stroke catching? The writer stutters as he speaks to the young nurse, who laughs. His mother is sitting up in bed, one eye under a patch, the other enlarged. Enormous. "Sorry," the writer says to the nurse. "Forgive me. Sometimes I have trouble with words." His mother's head slowly rotates to the right, the eye now taking them in. "You see," he continues, "English is actually my second language." His mother seems to begin to smile. "That's right, my second language. My first language was desire."

His mother in green housecoat, red exercise sponge in right hand. The doctor stops by. He's been her physician for some years, treats her with respect and affection, refers to her as "Mother" when speaking to her children. "Mother had a bad night," the doctor says.

He holds her hand. "I'm tempted to squeeze," she tells him.

"How are you today?"

"I think I'm going to be difficult if things continue like this."

Along the Charles in an ambulance, driver going way too fast. No emergency here, just a transfer. On a jump seat next to his mother, who's on her back, strapped to a gurney, the writer narrates their passage down Storrow Drive: Larz Anderson Bridge; Harvard Business School; Cottage Farm Bridge; the Esplanade; Community Boat Club; the curve near Charles Street Jail. Terra cognita: she's lived in Boston seventy-two of her seventy-four years.

In the hospital parking lot, attendants lift the gurney out of the ambulance, stand it on end by the Emergency Room door. The air is crystalline and very cold, sun right in his mother's face. She inhales deeply, once, twice, again, nostrils working to identify the many scents. They're almost at the harbor, ocean just beyond. "This is good," she says.

"How are you doing, Mother?" No response. "Mother, a conversation is defined as an exchange of words between two or more people."

Eyes still closed, she raises her brows. "I'm learning how uncomfortable you can be and still be getting well."

The writer tells his mother that he's typing a letter.

"Are you using the Hermes?" The Hermes is the typewriter she works at.

"Winged feet," he replies, feeling she'd rather he didn't use it.

"Metonymy," she says.

"That's what all adolescents crave. A sense of their own metonymy."

"Shame on you," his mother says.

Reading some of his mother's more bravura poems to her. "Benthic? For the love of God, what's the root?"

"Benthos."

"Oh."

"You realize," his mother says, "that poems in the form of an argument are already half-won." The writer thinks about it. "My poems aren't helping me here," she adds.

The night before yet another operation. "I don't believe Daddy would be of the same opinion," his mother says. A physician, he is ten years dead.

"Daddy would have felt this is too much?"

"Something like that."

"No, Mother, he wouldn't have liked it, but I'm positive he would feel this had to be done. Anyway, just think of the damn thing as a hop, skip, and a jump. Then we're through it."

"I don't see the advantage," his mother says.

Practicing without a license, the children do flower therapy. Fresia to smell. And amaryllis, surging, surging, to wrap fingers around. They also try forehead therapy—a palm on the brow—as Daddy always did to console.

"Mother, consider this." The writer guides her hand to the potting soil. "We've known each other almost forty years."

"What's shaking?" His mother shrugs. "Very Gallic," he says. A magazine with one of her poems just arrived in the mail. Not having seen this one, he reads it out loud.

## A PROSODY

Unless you have to begin
a sentence with it, death
is only a lower-case noun,
five-letter word at that,
longer than life, love
or terser call of need,
even than loss, void,
almost long enough
to qualify for breath
with which it rhymes and (not
exactly) slantly, health

"What do you think, Mother?"
"I think I used to be a poet," she replies.

"Mother is not likely to leave the hospital," the doctor tells the children. "Her decline these last weeks has been inexorable, measured in millimeters. Why this should be her lot I do not know."

"BE here now," Richard Alpert, a.k.a. Ram Dass, used to advise in the seventies, prospering from the apparently boundless capacity of grown humans to infantilize themselves. "Be here now." For the writer, the phrase has always epitomized the meretricious. And yet—are not the workings of God mysterious?—it has also stood as a reproach to a life of putting words on paper. That is to say, Dass notwithstanding, in his heart of hearts the writer believes there is such a thing as enlightenment. And, further, that this enlightenment inheres in a profound letting go. Whatever its insights and beauties, epiphanies to the contrary, writing is a form of materialism. All that hefting and hewing. "Be here now"? So much of the time, writing is being there then.

"YOU'RE a writer? You ought to write the story of my life." Thus spake an octogenarian whose selfishness gave new meaning to the axiom that the good die young. As the writer understood what he was hearing, the man wormed his way into the clothing business in the Depression. Figured out just how to flatter, insinuate, inveigle, had finally usurped the position of the owner's son. He'd "made a killing," married three times, always kept a woman "on the side". Had enjoyed the best of health, could even pass on some wisdom: "Don't get old, son."

But of course the writer wasn't hearing him right, was he? The man knew his whole story, had no qualms about telling every bit of it. "You just write it down," he'd say, "you just write it down."

≺ ≺ ≺

AFTER a hard winter, a flu that just wouldn't go away, the writer's doing warmup exercises, soon to attempt several remedial miles on the dirt track, when the actor rounds the turn nearby.

"Join you in another lap," the writer calls, waving back, resuming his stretching. "Fuck it," he mutters. "This hurts." He's consoled, however, by the prospect of someone to run with. Even better, the actor seems to abhor silence. In his mid-thirties but possessed of a boyish eagerness to please, he perenially tells story after story. Perfect, the writer thinks: anything to put one's mind elsewhere.

When the actor rounds the turn again, moving slowly, the writer joins him. "Just the pace," the writer says. He laughs, but chastises himself. No negative thoughts: it will be hard enough.

"So how's it going?" the writer adds. This said, he expects to do little more than nod, grunt the occasional affirmative, and lift his feet. The actor, a compulsive raconteur, will take care of the rest. Though his tales tend to monopolize conversation, they are seldom self-serving or, even, about himself: somebody's daughter got lost in the Sierra, someone else's father was mugged in New York City. Nor is there any effort to deceive: the actor never claims such experiences as his own. It is also true, however, that he narrates these sagas with detail he can't possibly have remembered hearing. Over time, though the listener may appreciate the actor's effort, the detail begins to undercut itself, leads to questions about the story's veracity even when literal truth is of no particular importance. The listener may then also start to wonder what stories are not being told. By the actor or, since his words so fill the air, by others. Yet it is also true, the writer thinks, trying to forget where he is and what he's asking of his body, that such stories do make time pass.

"Nancy and I are separated," the actor says.

"Oh," the writer responds, surprised by so terse and so personal a statement. "Sorry to hear that."

"She's seeing someone. Another lawyer. They worked on a case together."

"Sorry," the writer says again as they jog on slowly.

"I'm just trying to figure out how to stay sane. The kids are coming home from camp this week. I'll spend some time with them. I sublet a cottage in the hills. I suppose we'll get back together, but you never know. Lots of things happen between people. You remember, I moved out for a while a couple of years ago. I was seeing somebody."

"Oh, no, I don't think I knew that."

For several moments they trudge on in silence, first wisps of afternoon fog flying in across the bay, sun still beating down, smell of eucalyptus sweet and strong. Dear God, the writer says to himself, nothing now distracting him from a sense of the mass of his body and force necessary to propel it.

"The night Nancy told me was the worst," the actor says. "I went over to North Beach, worked my way through the bars there, propositioned about a hundred women. At some point, I passed out on one of those green wooden benches in Washington Square Park, then woke up around four staring up at the towers of Saints Peter and Paul. Now what, I asked myself. After stumbling around for what seemed like forever, I finally found my car, got the door unlocked, and curled up in the back seat. When I woke up again, the sun was out and there was a parking ticket on my windshield."

"Jesus," the writer says as they round the far turn once again. "What a story."

He barely gets the words out: each leg weighs a thousand pounds, his lungs burn, the word "STOP" is flashing on and off just in front of his eyes. Lifting one foot, then another, it occurs to the writer that of course the actor has told this saga before. And, since they are little more than acquaintances, has no doubt told it many times. To friends, neighbors, colleagues, siblings, fellow runners, his former lover. Even so, the writer thinks, perhaps the actor does know something about stories. Whatever his incessant narratives have precluded, whatever they've allowed, perhaps the actor really believes that words have the capacity to save. Perhaps for him a story is a kind of mantra: repeated again and again, it will have the power of prayer.

"Whatever's right," the writer mutters, aware that the words must be unintelligible but unable to summon further force.

"Did you say something?" the actor asks.

Come on, the writer says to himself. Try it again. "For Christ's sake, if you need to, keep talking."

"What?"

The writer musters all his strength. "Just keep talking."

"All right," the actor replies, as if unable to believe he's heard the writer correctly. "If you really want me to."

SOME writers work every day, or at least sit down at the typewriter. A form of communion, perhaps, or something approaching physical necessity, like the ballet dancer's daily barre. Anthony Trollope seems to have defined the limit of this approach, allocating himself a weekly quota of pages. Finishing a novel in the afternoon, he'd begin another the next morning. In this fashion he produced more than seventy volumes of fiction and nonfiction while working full time in the British postal system.

Other writers determinedly take time off after a book. To recover, or to experience something beyond the austere clarity of the writer's study. "Real life," for instance. The comparison here may be with the ballet dancer who begins to develop a craving for sweets. For the writer, the danger is in not finding the way back to the study, a risk every writer senses, perhaps most of all when out playing the writer.

POETRY, Nabokov says, began "when a cave boy came running back to the cave, through the tall grass, shouting as he ran, 'Wolf, wolf,' and there was no wolf. His baboon-like parents, great sticklers for the truth, gave him a hiding, no doubt, but poetry had been born—the tall story had been born in the tall grass." Nabokov also wrote that "Every great writer is a great deceiver, but so is that arch-cheat, Nature. . . . The writer of fiction only follows Nature's lead."

Writing and what Ozick calls "the rapture of deceit" (while also using the nouns distortion / misrepresentation / illusion / imposture / fakery and the verbs exaggerate / impersonate / usurp / despoil / insinuate / appropriate). Of Hemingway's rapturous deceits, Basil Bunting wrote that he was "entitled to his lies, and to live them as vividly as he dared, for a novelist must inhabit the people he invents to make them convincing." Nonetheless, for Bunting Hemingway's "chronic fantasy was unusually vulgar, the dream so popular with women and womanish men of a magnanimous bully." Further, even in the service of art Bunting could grant only a limited liar's license. That is, Hemingway's version of Ford Madox Ford in *A Moveable Feast* was for Bunting as cowardly and contemptible as any mortal's self-serving lie.

As a child, the writer often lied to his parents. A lie being, initially or up to a point, so much easier than the truth. A solution in which nothing need be given up, through which neither the expectations of others nor one's own hunger were disappointed, irreconcilable. Magic which required no more than the making up of a story. At age nine, for instance, the writer was given a marvelous Schwin bike but enjoined not to ride it in the street. *Not to ride it in the street.* Surely his parents understood that all the kids rode their bikes in the street. What, ride on the sidewalk, stop at every curb? But how turn down the bike? Or, how tell his parents the truth?

Years later, reading Alan Lelchuck's *Shrinking*, the writer was somewhat consoled: "the writer lives by his lying, tells the truth by his lying." Was consoled also when he read Rilke: "Transforming is not lying," the poet said.

✑ ✑ ✑

Hᴇ was working on his first book. He'd do six or seven drafts of a story on the Selectric, then take the manuscript to a typist. Having a clean draft, he found, gave him distance on what he'd been writing, made it surprisingly easy to spot flaws. There was of course the danger of being reluctant to tear into what might appear to be a finished product—and already paid for—but generally he'd take out a pen as soon as he got home. At some point, finally, the story would seem impenetrable. Obsidian. And that would be it.

One day he took a story he'd worked on for a month or so to the typist who'd already done much of the book. As usual, they agreed he'd return the next afternoon. When he did, she invited him in and walked back to her study to get the pages she'd prepared. To make a long story short: she couldn't find the pages, never found them, neither the draft nor what she'd typed. It took a while, but in the ensuing weeks he rewrote the story, finally concluded he'd come fairly close to the original.

From that point on, when he finished writing each day he'd head up to the local xerox shop. Often it would be rush hour and he'd have to wait for a machine. The place did land-office business, an apparently endless supply of nonagenarians prudently duplicating the papers in their safety deposit boxes. Nonetheless, always he'd go. He kept the Xerox on his desk, original in the trunk of his car, reasoning that if both house and car were lost at the same time he'd probably be in one or the other. And beyond caring.

"*I* LOVE you," he said. Neither of them was young: they both, as they sometimes teased each other, had "been around the block a couple of times."

She thought about it. "Tell me a story," she finally replied.

"All right, if you want. But what kind?"

"You know, what I'd really like is a story with words you never used before."

IN *Awakenings*, neurologist Oliver Sacks describes his work with a ward of survivors of a rare sleeping sickness. One patient, Leonard L., was for twenty years "completely speechless and completely without voluntary motion except for minute movements of the right hand. With these he could spell out messages on a small letter board. . . ." Despite his disabilities, Mr. L., a former graduate student, read constantly (someone else, apparently usually his mother, turned the pages), even wrote book reviews. As a boy he said he wanted to bury himself among books, a wish, Dr. Sacks writes, he had indeed fulfilled.

In 1969, when Dr. Sacks started Mr. L. on a course of the "wonder" drug L-DOPA, a remarkable transformation ensued: "The rigidity vanished from all his limbs, and he felt filled with an access of energy and power; he became able to write and type once again, to rise from his chair, to walk with some assistance, and to speak in a loud clear voice. . . ." Soon, however, it appeared that Mr. L. had come too much back to life, his hungers "transmogrified into insatiable passions and greeds," his body wracked with "sudden impulsions and tics of the eyes, grimaces, clickings, and lightning-quick scratchings." Desperate, Mr. L. began an autobiography. " 'It'll bring me together,' Mr. L. said; 'It'll chase out the devils. It'll bring everything into the full light of day.' " As Dr. Sacks writes, "Using his shrunken dystrophic index-fingers, Mr. L. typed out an autobiography 50,000 words in length, in the first three weeks of June. He typed almost ceaselessly, twelve or fifteen hours a day, and *when* he typed he indeed 'came together,' and found himself free from his tics and distractions, from the pressures which were driving and shivering his being; when he left the typewriter, the frantic, driven, ticcing palilalia would immediately assert its hegemony again."

While this endeavor at autobiography, what Sacks terms

"an act of supreme coherence and catharsis," unfortunately did not save Mr. L., the notion of integrating the self through writing has powerful appeal. Dr. Sacks himself, one gathers, is an inveterate if not compulsive writer. And one thinks of Virginia Woolf, her sense that as soon as she stopped writing she sank "down, down." And yet, we know Conrad said that writing, excluding "all that makes life really lovable and gentle," was like the "everlasting sombre stress of the westward journey around Cape Horn . . . a long desperate fray." And Tolstoy, we read, cried out for someone to finish *Anna Karenina* for him.

So. One is loath to disagree with the good doctor's interpretation of this case. Nonetheless, it may perhaps still be said that, had Leonard L. continued to write, particularly at so awesome a pace, he might at last have come to concur with W.H. Auden's lament: "Lord, teach me to write so well that I shall no longer want to."

NEARLY every morning when he's writing, usually by 7:15, he passes through the rear gate and then the front gate, gets into his car, drives five blocks to the local cafe, sits outside on a bench with his cappuccino, and skims the *San Francisco Chronicle*. Always he starts with the sports section, Red Sox box score during baseball season, Celtics game summary otherwise. Then he drives home, puts the house in order, and heads into his study.

An architect he knows who lives in lower Manhattan, on Canal Street, is also "self-employed" with an office "in the home." Each weekday morning the architect dons running gear, jogs the fifty blocks up to Grand Central Station, and spends a few minutes watching commuters pour in off the trains from the suburbs. Thus fortified, he jogs back to his loft, brews coffee, showers, and settles down to work.

IN the fall of 1965 the writer attended Yale Law School for a week. It might have been ten days, actually. He'd finished Harvard the previous June, and, like some of his classmates, had given little thought to what would come next. It was then à la mode to voice disdain for the legal profession: one was born for something finer. Nonetheless, he had no sense of alternative. Nor had he ever ventured into a coutroom or read the Constitution, though he did finally go to see one attorney, uncle of the woman he was dating. "Do you find the law a satisfying career?" he asked. Not wanting to jeopardize a jot of his potential, he believed this decision would determine the course of his life. "Satisfying?" the attorney responded. "It's a living." Even so, for want of having imagined something better or the courage to just do nothing at all, the writer packed his gear to move to New Haven, bought a new suit and London Fog raincoat at Stonestreet's on Mass. Avenue, right across from Widener Library.

He'd done his undergraduate thesis on Conrad's *Lord Jim*, had studied Conrad for Erik Erikson's class on the life cycle. Surely he knew Conrad had left Poland, wandered, sailed, attempted suicide, and become an officer in the British Merchant Marine, all before beginning to write—in English. Still, he had the notion that writers were born, not made, and that these authentics manifested their genius at an early age. Certainly Harvard had its share of the precocious, many of them not merely published but already in one camp or another, Lowell / Ginsberg / Warhol. He'd never set down a word of fiction, had just read, and even at that he was only a tyro. He did think he could write term papers well, but then the tutor supervising his senior thesis tore apart his first draft, blackening each page, filling the facing page with severe criticism. Hurt, the writer began a second draft determined to show he could compose sentences that were spare and true.

That spring he authored four short stories, his first—and for years, his last. One has a narrator, an expatriate living on the Riviera, whose voice not surprisingly resembles Marlow's in *Lord Jim*. The narrator ventures a friendship with a young traveler who, mourning a failed love affair, drowns himself. It should be noted that the girl the writer was dating wrote her thesis on Virginia Woolf. They'd also both been impressed by Truffaut's *400 Blows*, which closes with the protagonist trapped at the edge of the sea.

In each of the other three stories there is at least one death. A couple on a camping trip live through what appears to have been an atomic blast. She turns out to be pregnant, a good thing since they're the sole survivors. Another story seems an elaboration of Shelley's *Ozymandias*. The king constructs a great tomb (on the front of which is inscribed "Behold my works," etc.), then takes his own life in the story's last line. With the fourth of these sagas (terrible car crash, driver's best friend launched through the windshield), the writer's creative fever seemed to have consumed itself.

Several months later he went down to New Haven to begin law school, but there was that immortal soul of his not to waste. The Torts instructor lit into him the first class. Worse, his roommate had already annotated the semester's casework in various colors of Magic Marker. It looked like just three more years of competing, and for something he wasn't even sure he wanted. Now he knew he'd been crazy to come.

He was leaving, the writer told his classmates, many of whom seemed envious. "Where will you go?" asked the kind professor of Contracts, a German émigré. "Back to California, I guess." He'd been out there the summer before. "Oh, California," the professor replied. "Zat's where the action is."

So the writer left law school, but to do what? The ensuing years can in part be construed as his effort to replace the life he was unable to stop imagining he might have lived. And of course still he'd produced only those few stories, although now he thought of writing nonfiction. He'd read Erikson, Reisman, Oscar Lewis, Agee's *Let Us Now Praise Famous Men.* To see suffering first hand and live to tell the story, to excoriate those who refused to acknowledge what was true, now this might be worth doing.

Law school and the Eastern seaboard behind him, Vietnam war beginning to work its way home, the writer had departed a world in which white males were still being groomed to administer, where women were still far more likely to acknowledge the realm of the private. Callow and foolish, an utter mystery to himself, nonetheless the writer had a kind of agenda. Having taken this momentous-seeming step off the path of credentialing and public action, now he began to pick his way toward passion / vision / gossip / the intuitive / the unspoken, some of which was then ascribed to or found in the domain of women. Of course he sensed that writing would require much discipline, and that many men—and women—wrote for status, power, money. Nonetheless, as he now read his life, so long had he held himself in check that to admit these impulses—the need to quit school, the hunger to write—suggested a thousand others, implied, crazily, the end of "renunciation," "postponed gratification," and, even, "law and order." Scary, scary, to see all limits receding, but to have continued as before? Oh, well, he would have suffocated, would have been a dead man. Or so, heart pounding, he told himself, truly believed.

By 1967, world so full of change and strife, having been in California more than a year and repudiated much of his past, the writer stopped in one day at the office of the *San Francisco Express Times,* an "underground" paper. Marvin Garson was the editor, the enterprise funded by wife Barbara Garson's play *MacBird,* an anti–Lyndon Johnson tract. Sitting down across from a friend who was writing for the paper, Marvin nearby, the office little more than a garage with a few chairs and desks, the writer began to "rap" about his recent trip to Big Sur as they smoked some marijuana. Finally, Marvin said, "You ought to write that down."

"Why?"

"I'll print it, that's why."

Thus the writer's first published story was about Billy the shoemaker, a "short, thin, forked radish of a man"; Zeke, who wore hand shears at his side "like a Burbankian Billy the Kid"; and other inmates of the Gorda Mountain community. "Most people who pass through the life of the mountain," he wrote, "are willy-nilly participating in a great work of oral literature. This usually commences with simple questions, such as, 'Do you remember that crazy motherfucker so-and-so?', or, 'Do you remember when that crazy motherfucker did such-and-such?' " The writer also had a vision of Billy as curator of the asylum, a mad Aesop "breathing life into memories."

The August 14, 1968, issue of the *Express Times* contained pieces on the Black Panthers, Huey Newton, various uprisings and teach-ins, a feature on Minnesota Fats, and Big Sur. "Got any more?" Marvin, high on mescaline, asked the next time he came into the office. Before the writer forgot his ambition to emulate Chaucer and swept himself away in another direction entirely, imagining himself a combination of Zorro and Che, before he concluded, like Ken Kesey, that it's better to be a lightning rod than a seismograph, he wrote another twenty pieces for Marvin. Each week he'd wait for the paper to be delivered to the office, generally taking a stack and heading for North Beach to sell them on the corner of Broadway and Columbus, standing in front of the Condor, Carol Doda's silicon breasts earning big money just behind him. He'd argue with the tourists about drugs or the war in Vietnam, shock the bourgeoisie, urge them to read his latest. Just twenty-four, he had oh-so-many-hungers, was utterly beyond his own control, but at times really thought he might become a writer. Someday, someday, if the madness would only die down, if there'd just be a bit of a pause before the next apocalypse. Then, *then* he'd seek the path of the heart, sing the lives of his fellow pilgrims.

JOUBERT was not a writer of maxims in the traditional French manner. He was something far more difficult to define: a writer who spent his whole life preparing himself for a work that never came to be written. . . .
Paul Auster

From his early youth [Joubert] was interested in nothing but literature and writing. As a very young man he was close friends with Diderot, and later with Restif de la Bretonne, both prolific writers. As a grown man his friends were almost exclusively famous authors whose literary interests he shared and who, well aware of the quality of his mind and style, tried to coax him out of his silence. And he certainly had no difficulty in expressing himself: his extensive, far-ranging correspondence denotes the ease and facility so characteristic of his century, but enhanced here by the subtlety of thought and manner proper to a man who relishes words and who excels in manipulating them. Yet this exceptionally gifted man who was always scribbling in his notebook, never published anything and left nothing his contemporaries considered worth publishing.
Maurice Blanchot

Writing is closer to thinking than to speaking.
Deprived for a long time of ideas that suited my mind or of a language that suited my ideas.
*Yes* and *no* are not precisely clear words, but definite words. In clear words, there is more light than movement or attitude.
Ordinary brightness is no longer enough for me—when the meaning of words is not as clear as their sound—that is, when they do not offer to my thought objects as transparent in themselves as the terms that name them.
I stop when I see no more light; it is impossible for me to write by feeling my way.
I confess that I am like an aeolian harp—which gives off some pretty sounds but can play no songs.

Tormented by the cursed ambition always to put a whole book in a page, a whole page in a sentence, and this sentence in a word. I am speaking of myself.

I would like thoughts to succeed one another in a book like stars in the sky, with order, with harmony, but effortlessly and at intervals, without touching, without mingling.

Joubert

"When your book comes out," she said, "you'll be famous. You'll leave me."

WHY write? Sometimes simply because the story must be told. For instance . . . Though the writer has lived in northern California fifteen of the last twenty years, still there are things which seem better done back East. Such as buying clothes. On yet another return to Boston, for example, he barely survived the memorial celebration of his mother's life and work wearing a twenty-two-year-old summer suit. Inhaling to get into it, he swore a blood oath to purchase a new one if the buttons would just hold for the next few hours.

Sad to say, he returned to California before he could go shopping. Soon after, he drove over to the Democratic Convention in San Francisco on the strength of a borrowed press pass. Mondale / Mondale / Mondale, Hart soon to concede. It took less than an hour to conclude this wasn't the show for him. Riding back up the Moscone Center's escalator to street level, passing police and demonstrators, the writer drifted toward Union Square. The whole area was nearly empty of human life, locals scared off by the threat of crowds from the convention. Browsing as he meandered, seeing salesmen standing idle in vacant stores, the writer remembered his oath. Brooks Brothers seemed a prudent choice, but as it happened they had no summer suits in June. OK, he could live with that. He walked past Neiman Marcus, but remembering how people say "Needless Markup," kept on going. Then he reached Wilkes Bashford. The prices, he was startled to see, began at around five hundred dollars, but the store's real character appeared to be defined by the thousand-dollar range. And the styles? Well, the suits were Italian. "Are you Italian?" people sometimes ask the writer. He has dark hair, eyes, tans easily. "Yes," he answers, "but I was raised by two Jews. My parents." This joke is of course older than he is, but it came to mind as he walked out of Wilkes Bashford. They have a bar there, free drinks for customers. But not Italian, unable even to get his arms all the way through the sleeves, having saved—and so feeling as though he'd actually earned—a thousand dollars more or less not including tax and alterations, the writer felt absolutely no pain heading out the door stone cold sober.

Now, he wouldn't have experienced any of this in Boston. He'd have shopped in Harvard Square at the Coop or J. Press, buying something Ivy League, a suit just like the one he'd purchased twenty-two years before. Or, feeling flush, he'd have gone down past Copley Square to see what they had at Louis or at Martini Carl, places he remembers his father going to. Which brings us to the story that seems to demand telling. Several years ago, in 1983, perhaps, back in Boston yet another time, the writer stopped by Martini Carl. Martini Carl's? Improbable either way, once you think about it. In any case, while browsing that day he saw a pair of boots, tried them on, liked them. At the register he gave the clerk his VISA card.

"Hey," the man said, "you related to the cancer doctor?"

"One of his children," the writer replied. It felt good, being home again.

"Is that right? The hospital over there, it's really something. All those kids. You must be proud."

"I am, thank you."

"You know, I was just saying to myself the other day I haven't seen your father around much lately. He been out of town?"

The writer thought it over. Why bother? But then he responded, "My father died in 1973."

Though he seemed to have no doubt that the writer was in fact his father's son, the clerk nonetheless missed nary a beat:

" '73? Naa. You got to be kidding. Naa. No way."

APPARENTLY no subscriber to the notion of fiction as disinformation, a friend once says he's amazed how much the writer divulges in his prose. Not simply what appears patently autobiographical, but, persistently, a kind of knowledge which implicates the writer as much as any character.

The writer thinks it over. His friend seems not to understand that people may reveal only what is not vital to protect. Or that revelation can be a need. Or that life may simply be impossible to conceal. For instance, that day his friend carries an extra seventy-five pounds, has large rings under his eyes, can't stop picking at a scab on his forearm, is wearing a shirt with circus motif—trapeze artists, elephant dancers, and lion tamers—cut à la Errol Flynn in *Captain Blood,* meanwhile narrating a saga of self-justification and self-reproach on themes including being overweight, his children's college tuition, the price of a new BMW, his latest career move, the Red Sox's pennant hopes, his wife's inattention.

No, the writer says to himself, privacy is never absolute. And as for his friend? Hmm. At that particular moment his life seems . . . Well, yes. An open book.

"IT is nothing new," writes Anne Carson, "to say all utterance is erotic in some sense, that all language shows the structure of desire at some level. Already in Homer's usage, the same verb *(mnaomai)* has the meaning 'to give heed, to make mention' and also the meaning 'to court, to woo, be a suitor.' Already in ancient Greek myth, the same goddess (Peithō) has charge of rhetorical persuasion and the arts of seduction. Already in earliest metaphor, it is 'wings' or 'breath' that move words from speaker to listener as they move eros from lover to beloved."

Writing and eros. The technique of writing, George Graq argues, "has to do with the slow and patient skill of the erotic." And of his work, Tennessee Williams maintained, "I can't write a story unless there is at least one character in it for whom I have physical desire." But even if the act of writing does not imply the erotic, surely books can. "If I were a man," Edna O'Brien says, "having written exactly what I, as a woman, have written, I would have waiting for me in the wings of the world many, many willing, adoring, women."

Of Yeats, Seamus Heaney wrote: "If the act of mind in the artist has all the intentness and amourousness and every bit as much of the submerged aggression of the act of love, then it can be maintained that Yeats's artistic imagination was often in a condition that can only be properly described as priapic." Actually, not just his artistic imagination: for Yeats, poetic inspiration and sexual impulse were integrally related. According to Richard Ellmann, at age sixty-eight, his sexual powers diminished, Yeats learned that an Austrian physiologist had developed an operation for sexual rejuvenation. Apparently, the brief operation (also performed on Sigmund Freud) was what we now know as a vasectomy. Nonetheless, Yeats felt restored, both continued to enjoy sexual intimacy and to experience renewed literary productivity in what he referred to as his second puberty.

In one poem from this five-year period before his death, "The Circus Animals' Desertion," Yeats returns again to the relationship of art and sexual passion, theme of his earlier Byzantium poems, and seems initially to be celebrating what Ellman calls "the purifying and distancing power of art." Ellman argues, however, that Yeats is in fact moving toward a quite different conclusion:

> Those masterful images because complete
> Grew in pure mind, but out of what began?
> A mound of refuse or the sweepings of a street,
> Old kettles, old bottles, and a broken can,
> Old iron, old bones, old rags, that raving slut
> Who keeps the till. Now that my ladder's gone,
> I must lie down where all the ladders start,
> In the foul rag-and-bone shop of the heart.

REVIEWS. Even Nobel Prize winners, Philip Roth writes, "despite Their Great Contribution to Humanity . . . might not object if their critics were pelted with offal while being drawn down Fifth Avenue in cages." Roth apparently tries to be out of the country when reviews appear. Gogol did the same. As Henri Troyat explains, Gogol "wanted to hear every last one, but he preferred to receive them weakened by their long trajectory." A prudent strategy, it would seem, given the helpless rage of the stay-at-home. "I am sitting in the smallest room in my house," Max Reger wrote a critic. "I have your review in front of me. Soon it will be behind me."

"That's the story that convinced me to give your collection a good review," a critic once said to the writer when they met at a party. "It's the best story in the book."

You mean, the one you like the best, the writer said to himself, trying not to bite the hand that feeds.

AT Memorial Stadium in Baltimore several years ago to see the Orioles play Kansas City, after a few innings of beer the writer took a break to go to the men's room. Rounding a corner, walking toward a bank of urinals, he encountered a graffito on the facing wall: *Suck My White Nuts Porch Monkey.* Back in the grandstand, the writer saw green grass against dark sky, heard the murmur, roar, of the crowd, downed peanuts, munched soft-shell crab. Night advancing, the writer recalled that some people consider language a reflection of the fundamental spiritual nature of the world. For the Kabbalists, for instance, speech reaches God because it comes from God.

Years before, the summer he turned thirteen, the writer spent eight weeks at a venerable prep school not far from Boston. One of his teachers was a very short Londoner. The first day of class, dressed in tweed coat, school tie, and gray flannel pants despite a temperature in the nineties and high humidity, he claimed to have once slipped into the armor of Edward the Sixth. Or some tiny English Edward murdered in the Tower or buried in Westminster. Having so quickly broached and put off-limits the question of his size, he spent the rest of the summer hazing the students, all of whom without virtue were already far taller than he was. Product of the English public school system, the teacher had an expertise in tactics of humiliation that matched his need to dominate such callow adversaries. Ox. Bloody ox. Lummox. Cretin. Mooncalf. Dolt. Are you struck dumb, man? And so on. The writer spent each weekday lunchtime staring at the ice-cream scoop of potato salad on his plate, struggling to memorize yet another poem for the class. A poem a day, every day. The terror was in being called on, being driven to tears. "Full fathom five my father lies. . . ." "Where the bee sucks there suck I. . . ."

Even then the writer understood that nothing the boys were could warrant such contempt. This though no observer would have described them as strangers to the practice of malice, though they all had the adolescent's abhorence of one's own weakness in others, gladly identified with the aggressor whenever possible, would have done so in class had the Englishman allowed such familiarity.

Session ended, the writer took the train home. Time passing, sealing off this kind of childhood experience, the writer seldom thought about the class. But then one night when he was forty-two, he had a dream in which he was saying, "Language is love, language is love." Bright and early the next morning, as if to remedy a half-truth, his memory served up the summer he was thirteen.

◿ ◿ ◿

D<small>URING</small> their courtship, exploring the unmapped terrain between them, English sometimes intolerably explicit, they occasionally express a sentiment in French. For instance, trying for the first time to tell her the obvious—that he likes her very much—he says, *"Oh, comme je t'aime."* In the same period they also create between them a kind of conditional mode—in English—frequently referring to themselves or each other by the indefinite pronoun. As in, "Someone's thinking of taking a trip to Oaxaca. Is anybody interested in going?" Or, again seeing the roses she's given him in the vase by his bed, unwilling to ask who else he might be dating, she says, "Oh, someone's been giving you flowers." To which he replies, ducking the Ur-question, teasing her with the ambiguity, "Yes, someone."

Several thousand years before they met, a poet sang of a much-turned and many-turning man who's having a hard time making his way home. At one resting place in this apparently interminable journey, his host asks him to speak of his travels. Though the guest, the resourceful Odysseus, professes to doubt that recounting such a woeful story will improve his spirits, he begins to relate what has befallen him since leaving Troy. As he explains, after stopping at the land of the Lotus-Eaters the Achaeans came to the cave of the Cyclops Polyphemus and asked for his hospitality. The monster, however, snatched up "Two of my comrades as if they were puppies and dashed them / Down at his feet where their brains ran out on the ground. / Then he cut them up and prepared his evening meal, / Which he ate like a mountain lion—meat, bones, / Entrails and all." The next morning, Polyphemus consumed two more of Odysseus's men, then sealed the mouth of the cave that was his home with an enormous rock, leaving Odysseus "Brooding evil in the darker cave of my heart. . . ." When the monster returned that night, Odysseus got him drunk and then said,

"Cyclops, you ask my name,
A famous name, and I will tell it to you,
That you may give me the friendly gift you promised.
Nobody is my name. They all call me Nobody—
My mother, my father, and all the rest of my friends."

When the monster passed out, Odysseus and his men took a great stake and plunged it into his single eye, spinning it about until "the burning / Blood oozed out around it."

When the other Cyclopes, who lived nearby, heard Polyphemus' screams, they called, "Is somebody rustling / Your flocks or actually killing you by force / Or some trick?" To which Polyphemus responded, "O friends, Nobody is killing me." Not surprisingly, the other monsters said that if "nobody is hurting you / You must be sick, and sickness you cannot escape. . . ."

Hearing this, his revenge achieved, the wily Odysseus laughed. What a game language was. And what a weapon he'd made of the indefinite pronoun.

∢ ∢ ∢

A SOPHOMORE in college, the writer was convinced happiness would follow as soon as he found the right major. English? Or something more practical, Economics, for example. Or something less practical: Classics, Celtic. For his friend Alex, however, it was high time to paint, write, play guitar. Picasso and Henry Miller his guides, Alex concluded college had nothing more to offer him. Moving to Cambridgeport—six rooms for forty dollars, no phone, and a note pad on the door—perennially dressed in khaki pants, white T-shirt, and white Oxford shirt with tail out, sporting flip-flops in warm weather, Alex ceased to measure his life in semesters. Soon, inspired by Dylan and the Beatles, he began to compose songs.

The humid, opulently slow summer of 1966, just before the writer headed west in his red VW bug. A year past his B.A., he'd dropped out of law school, taught college for a semester, taken some graduate courses, achieved part-time work as a janitor in a Harvard Square architect's office. Smoking cigarettes, smoking marijuana, he and Alex sang songs from *Rubber Soul*—"Norwegian Wood," "In My Life"—and emulated the harmonies of the Mamas and Papas, Alex's red hair ever longer, his extraordinarily thin face large with laughter. Often they drove to Somerville in the middle of the tropical night for another load of just-baked honey-dipped donuts. The writer broke up with one girl, fell in love with another. Watched Alex yet again adjust his capo, search for his flat pick.

Alex was a clear spirit. And tough. The objections of his parents? Well, they had their views. But so did he. Alex was also more than willing to pay the price of his beliefs. Delayed action yields delayed solutions, he liked to say. The esteem of others? Only freedom was something he feared losing.

By the time the writer finished his first book, Alex had already put together an album, traipsed down to New York with the tape, sold it, and won the right to be his own producer. Then, feeling he'd outgrown Cambridge, deciding against New York, Alex moved to Los Angeles. In 1972, visiting southern California, the writer again spent some time with Alex. They drove out to see Spahn Ranch, where Manson had roamed. Met a psychic, who predicted California would tumble into the Pacific within a year. Walked down Sunset Boulevard, where Alex spotted Ann-Margret. "Who's she?" the writer asked, not yet an Angeleno.

Living in a cottage in a modest corner of Hollywood, beset by noisy and potentially dangerous neighbors, Alex had various possibilities developing in and around film and records but was without certain income or status. And while he continued to live austerely, a bohemian life in the face of Los Angeles' dazzling materialism seemed perilously close to mere lack of money.

As he drove north the writer wondered if Alex would be tough enough for southern California. New York, he thought, would have been simpler: it seemed that just calling oneself an artist still counted for something there. Of course, his interest in Alex's future spoke for more than concern abut the well-being of a friend. Alex had set an example for the writer, shown him a possibility the writer then recognized in himself. One book out, thinking of trying another, still unsure of his vocation, the writer needed Alex to make it.

*E*ARLY December in Paris. End of the afternoon. Gray, cold. Wine and cheese on the cafe table, two six-foot Senegalese women tending bar several feet beyond.

Just forty-one, a successful documentary film maker, she's lived with a young English writer the last several years. From the start she believed in his gift, encouraged him, found him a sinecure, helped him obtain a work permit, recently sent his novel to an editor she knows in the States, is certain it will be published. Three nights ago they celebrated his twenty-seventh birthday. The night before last he told her he was moving out.

"It's been living hell," she says in her accented English. "And then I heard that my father is very sick. And this morning I lost my keys. Perfect, no?" She crushes her Gitane, exhales. "Of course it had to happen. I knew it all along. Even last summer in Greece, when things were so wonderful." She brightens, puts both hands behind her neck, pushes up her hair.

"How could you be so sure it wouldn't work?"

"Because it was obvious."

"But why? Because he's young?"

"No, no, that's not it. The thing is, I always knew he'd want to be with other women. That he'd have to be with them."

"But why? Are you saying you think that's how men are?"

"No. He's not like other men I've known. He has a real passion. He's going to be a fine writer some day. A great writer, perhaps. That's why I knew sooner or later it would end. I knew he'd have to be with other women. Because of his work. Because of his art."

"But aren't there writers, men or women, who can work well only because they stay with the same mate, have that love, history, stability?"

"Maybe so," she says, "but not him. He's the other kind."

*H*OW can actors memorize so many lines?
How can dancers spin without getting dizzy?
How can writers spend so much time alone?

THEY'D met; they really liked each other. But how much to say? "I'm falling for you," the writer finally told her.

She grinned. "What's that supposed to mean?"

"Why don't you look it up?"

Going into his study, she opened the old Webster's New International, Second Edition, that he kept by his desk.

"Ready?"

"Ready."

"*Fall for.* It appears here after fall flat and before fall out, as in, to have a falling out."

"Thanks for the information."

"Sorry. I thought you were the one who loved words."

"I confess: for years I've been having an affair with them."

"I suppose I should be jealous. I suppose. Should I?"

"Do you mind?"

"All right. Relax. Here we go. '*Fall for:* To take a fancy to (a person or thing) with enthusiastic abandon. . . .' "

"There it is. Finally."

"Wait a second, wait a second: '. . . also, to be deceived by.' Well?"

"Well what?"

"What do you think?"

"Fucking English. Fucking language."

SHORTY and Al cruise on down to the white boy's cell. "Hey, home," Shorty says, "what you up to anyway? Writin' again? Sheuut, you know the Man just gonna tear that up, put your ass in isolation." Shorty waits for some response, waits a little longer. "Hey, you hear me?"

Shorty checks the boy out once more. "Lookee there, Alfred," Shorty says, "too busy to talk. Hope to die: a real-life writin' fool. Come on, Alfred, come on: you tell me there aren't all different ways to do time."

OVER a period of fifteen years, painter Andrew Wyeth recently announced, he produced several hundred drawings and paintings of model Helga Testorf without disclosing their existence even to his wife. This allegedly concealed work, critics now suggest, may also have been the source of and influence on his other, public, work. Whatever the actual history of these paintings and drawings, Wyeth seems always to have been what he calls "a secretive bastard," believing that to talk about work in progress is to destroy it, regretting only his inability to extend the privacy that enables his art: "I wish I could paint without me existing—that just my hands were there."

As for the writer: of course the manuscript is to become a book, people will read it. But work-in-progress, one's notes. The writer has file cabinets that lock, closets with hasps and locks, can lock the doors to each room. Lives in a kind of Carcassonne, all walls and turrets.

The pleasure of leaving folders out in his study, free from prying eyes. And yet: the cat approaches while he's writing, jumps up onto the desk, hunches on the manuscript. There can be no blame: living things are drawn to the flame of privacy.

No doubt the writer's problems this particular afternoon—sitting at the typewriter, elbow aching, sky bright blue out the window—stem from reading too much as a child. *Make Way for Ducklings;* Richard Halliburton's *Book of Marvels; Robin Hood* by Howard Pyle; Dr. Spock on babies; William Bradford Huie's *The Revolt of Mamie Stover;* the National Geographic ("Quick, take off your blouse, here comes the . . ."); Kerouac's *On the Road.* The primrose path. Vargas Llosa writes that one recurring theme in fiction is the risk of taking books literally. Don Quixote, poor man, is inspired by tomes on chivalry. And Emma Bovary, for whom things end so badly, has read too many romances.

Earlier in the day, the writer's goddaughter Cordelia and her stepsister Miranda were visiting. Delia's parents had been separated more than ten years, but her father had recently joined her mother and grandmother at the Mexican border. He'd never met his wife's mother before: she'd refused to meet him because he was black. Now she was dying of cancer, having searched in vain for a miracle cure, and he'd offered to help by driving them north to home.

But all that, as they say, is another story. Sitting in the living room with Cordelia and Miranda, the writer was speaking about Lear, Goneril, Regan, about Prospero, Ariel, Caliban. Pulling out his copy of *The Tempest,* he turned to the passage in which Prospero, having used supernatural powers to regain his rightful place in the world, is about to leave exile for his dukedom. Renouncing the magic which had once cost him temporal power, after this dazzling display of visions, illusions, masques, and songs, Prospero says:

> . . . I have bedimmed
> The noontide sun, called forth the mutinous winds,
> And 'twixt the green sea and the azured vault

> Set roaring war: to the dread rattling thunder
> Have I given fire, and rifted Jove's stout oak
> With his own bolt; the strong-based promontory
> Have I made shake, and by the spurs pluck'd up
> The pine and cedar: graves at my command
> Have waked their sleepers, oped, and let 'em forth
> By my so potent Art. But this rough magic
> I here abjure . . .
> . . . I'll break my staff
> Bury it certain fathoms in the earth,
> And deeper than did ever plummet sound
> I'll drown my book.

Sitting there with Delia and Miranda, the writer explained that some readers construe this passage as Shakespeare's farewell to art, a repudiation of his poetic power, his reentry into the sphere of ordinary life. Such readers, the writer told them, also like to read the Epilogue as Shakespeare's envoi to the theater, to imagine Shakespeare himself playing the part of Prospero, stepping forward at the end of this magic show to address an audience that over the years has seen so many displays of his almost supernatural powers.

Glancing at the text, the writer remembered being seventeen in Harry Levin's English 123. Two semesters of Shakespeare, six plays each semester. Reading *The Tempest* again and again, euphoric with his sense of the artist as master of illusion. Undaunted by the anomalies of art suggested by the monster Caliban: "You taught me language; and my profit on't is, I know how to curse." (Undaunted also, that year, by the humiliation Ingmar Bergman made his troupe of "artists" suffer in *The Magician.*)

Cordelia and Miranda shifting restlessly, Ariel (sic) the cat popping through the cat door, the writer read them the Epilogue:

> Now my charms are all o'erthrown,
> And what strength I have's mine own,

Which is most faint. Now 'tis true
I must be here confined by you,
Or sent to Naples. Let me not,
Since I have my dukedom got
And pardoned the deceiver, dwell
On this bare island by your spell;
But release me from my bands
With the help of your good hands.
Gentle breath of yours my sails
Must fill, or else my project fails,
Which was to please. Now I want
Spirits to enforce, art to enchant;
And my ending is despair
Unless I be relieved by prayer,
Which pierces so that it assaults
Mercy itself and frees all faults.
As you from crimes would pardoned be,
Let your indulgence set me free.

OF course, writing as control: to remake the world, or to be the one telling—and so determining—"the story." Also, the book as a given. Take it or leave it. But what of writing as a plea to be heard? Presuming, necessitating, a willing other. Or writing as immersion in an element, perforce requiring a yielding to its possibilities, demands. Writing as submission.

EARLY in 1975, the writer very much wanted a credit card. His written application—form picked up at the cash register of a Chinese restaurant, plastic holder next to the abacus—having been denied, he went to his bank, spoke with the manager. Strike one, drastic fluctuations of income, construed as a liability even after the writer explained that such variation allowed income averaging. Strike two: self-employed. (The writer did not add that in his view just about every waking act was tax-deductible.) "And the source of your income?" the manager asked. "Books?" Strike three.

Daunted but determined, the writer explained that he had a savings account in this branch, didn't even want the card as a credit instrument, merely sought to avoid lugging around hundred-dollar bills.

"What about your credit rating?"

"I don't think I have one."

"You must. Haven't you ever bought anything on time?"

"Never. My father always told us to avoid debt."

"You own a car?"

"Yes."

"But you own it outright?"

"Yes." The writer didn't add that it was a '65 Olds Cutlass convertible, gift from his brother, one hundred and ten thousand miles on the engine, a top that was ever less automatic. And sporting, blow-torched in enormous letters down the length of the driver's side, the inscription IMPEACH FORD.

Victory at sea. On the strength of his savings account, the writer got a card, credit limit two hundred and fifty dollars. So there he was, thirty going on thirty-one, the once-young of the whole damn country crawling in on their bellies from the bitter end of the sixties. Credentialing, getting MBA's. Love now a five-letter word, spell it m-o-n-e-y. And the writer? Living by his wits. Violating the seasons. Pursuing a craft, a vision. Still on the road. His friends settled down, grown up, writer stuck in some earlier stage of development, feeling, during the reentry shock and dislocation between books, kin to gypsies, disabled war veterans, refugees, unskilled unemployables, victims of forced early retirement. Given a kind of niche in this brave new world as first one book and then another was published, but in fact utterly off the grid of born-again materialism. Walking a kind of fiduciary tightrope, making absolutely certain not to look down. And finding himself, suddenly, possessor of a credit card. Business card soon to follow, $9.53 for the first thousand.

OVER the years, the writer's never lost a root curiosity about the fate of people he's known, a curiosity which usually reaches his inner ear in the language of his childhood: "What ever happened to him?"; "What did she do with her life?"; "What did he make of himself?" Though such curiosity of course has a component of self-appraisal, there's also simply the sheer hunger to know. Sometimes, now, considering the various turns his own life may still take, or wondering if in fact the pattern is long since clear to anyone with the eyes to see, the writer asks, "What is my story?" And, when times have been hard: "What will become of me?"

THE writer had a friend in college who took a year off in what was then Tanganyika to help black refugees from South Africa. After coming home to finish his B.A., he joined the Peace Corps, for much of the next several years working with the Turkana up around Lake Rudolph. Back in Oregon to complete his pre-med requirements, he simply could no longer handle so much time indoors. Having spent summers on his uncles' ranches until going east to college, he now decided to travel to New Zealand to study advanced pasture management technique. Returning to the hill country of southwestern Oregon with a Border collie pup, he lived on a mountaintop with the dog and his horse, working as a hired hand until the downpayment on a place of his own could be arranged.

The writer's first visit, soon after the rancher took possession, they dug the hole for a new septic system in an unassuming but soaking rain. The system was comprised of two fifty-gallon oil drums, several trenches running down and away, and yeast. Now a cowboy, the writer drove to town and bought a pair of rubber boots. That first visit he also learned to take foul-weather gear with him no matter how blue the sky, got a bad case of poison oak, watched—and listened to—the slow death of a neighbor's cow. Just before heading south to California, he rode into the high country on roundup, horsemen climbing slowly in the morning fog, dogs out ahead, sun breaking through as they reached the prairie, all of them suddenly at a gallop when the dogs flushed not cattle but elk.

Over the next five years the writer made a number of long stays with the rancher and his wife, generally surviving perhaps most of the morning's work before heading in for a nap. Fencing, logging, shoeing a horse, hauling hay bales. Lambs and calves being birthed, doctored, culled, lugged, slaughtered. "Putting down" a dog kicked by a bull. Standing in the rain outside a dairy barn knee-deep in muck, mud, and manure, rancher and dairyman circumlocuting around the question of a piece of equipment that might or might not be loaned or borrowed.

Outsider in country where books were not much in evidence, novice where the unit of measure was handling machines and animals, the writer was repeatedly impelled to dislocate himself, to give up the security of his own terrain to learn about ranch life. He also sensed that the understanding he sought might be simply a function of time invested. Occasionally, a week passing, then another, he'd feel like a kind of litmus: exposed to ranch life, he'd see the change recorded in himself.

Slowly, certain things came clear. One day he finally read the pattern of the ranch's seasons: mechanical work in winter, when moving around the hill country was difficult; lambing in January; calving in March; doctoring in May; shearing in June; preparing for market, haying, fencing, and logging in summer and fall; doctoring the cattle again and weaning calves before the heavy rains and cold resumed. Another time, yet again walking past the weatherworn corrals and pens, he suddenly appreciated the terrible inevitability of the pattern, how ruthlessly the bellowing animals were funnelled toward all that prodding, tagging, branding, worming, fluking, trimming, cutting.

It took a number of years, but then the writer made a trip north and announced to the rancher and his wife that this time he wouldn't be helping out. He might have told them he'd be hindering. For the next week and more he stayed right with the rancher, asking questions, making notes. Even when the answer seemed obvious, he insisted on an explanation. What? Why now? The writer also began to read through the shelf of his friends' texts on progressive pasture management. Questions, reading: he'd adopted this more active mode of trying to apprehend—to grasp—the ranch, an approach which seemed entirely consonant with a life forever requiring mastery of yet another tool or technique. And without hesitation the writer focused on the material, certain that through it he'd arrive at matters of the spirit. "Consider a legume like clover," he later wrote, "which fixes nitrogen through nodules in its roots. Bacteria in the nodules put that nitrogen into the soil. As the clover develops, it provides enough nitrogen to make the rye, fescue, and orchard grass produce well. If sheep are then grazed intensively, they not only crop the grasses, which thrive on being driven hard, but their manure—more nitrogen!—keeps the clover and grasses growing. This means winter pasture growth, just what the ewes need when lambing. Richer milk. Healthier lambs. Ultimately not only is nothing lost, but a self-tending system of ever-greater plenitude develops."

If, over time, the writer could see that the pretty yellow flowers of tansy ragwort, so poisonous to cattle, were under assault by orange and black cinnabar-moth caterpillars, that the tansy was not poisonous to sheep, that the rancher used a pudbar to tamp nitroglycerin into the stump, that wethers are male lambs eunuched by an Elastrator, he was also coming to perceive the ranch itself as a force. Two thousand acres, seven hundred animals, and loan payments, the ranch's imperatives were incessant, and incessantly invoked. Further, it often appeared that nothing was without a function. So much being bred, sold, and consumed, even people sometimes seemed no more than another product, another element in the food chain.

Formidable as the ranch was, the writer nonetheless found it necessary to revise his sense of the hill country as remote and therefore safe. Coyotes tunnelled under fences; bear and elk could go over or through them. And then there were the humans. "Hunters," he later wrote, "crazily overarmed, drinking heavily, crossed property lines at will. Skidding and winching up impossible slopes, eroding prairies and rutting out roads, loaded rifles pointed out the windows. Eager for their quota, often shooting even in a heavy fog at any sound or movement."

The writer was also reappraising the language of the hill

country. Initially he'd been drawn to the ranchers' abiding reserve. Of course he'd seen Shane, read *The Virginian.* Such composure, economy of gesture, and taciturnity seemed from another century: gallant, courtly, southern, so ornate and formal and evasive as to be almost comic. Time passing, however, the writer came to feel that the style was in fact functional, structured for an avoidance of direct requests and refusals. No one, he came to believe, wanted to talk straight. To do so was to risk giving offense, and barns, for example, were just too easily burned.

Five years after his first visit to the ranch, hungry now both to describe this world and to explore whatever conclusions he might be moving toward, the writer was at the edge of fiction. Since he was still an outsider in hill country, it is perhaps no surprise that the protagonist of his story proved to be someone who comes to a ranch for a visit but then stays. And, since the writer was an outsider where books were if not feminine then simply beyond the realm of the masculine, it is also perhaps no surprise that his protagonist is a woman who marries a rancher. Who is, in time, overwhelmed by the relentless materialism of ranch life. Who seems finally to be asking: "Why ranch?"

Unanswerable, this question, subversive. As the writer shaped his story, however, rivalling in his inexorable naming the imperatives of hill country—digging a ditch here, felling a tree there, so to speak—often he had the feeling that in her question he was examining his own impulses. Sometimes he felt himself asking, Why so much force to render this brutal world? Why such commitment to the relentless specificity of prose? Why not, say, simply the occasional line of haiku?

ONCE there was a young woman who'd caught the writer's eye. Telling her he'd be out of town for a month, he left a copy of his book of stories in her mailbox. On his return he dialed her number. Love my book / love me, he said to himself as the phone rang. "Hi," she replied exuberantly when she heard his voice. "This is a real coincidence. I just now started your stories. I would have got to them sooner but I had another book to finish first, and I'm a slow reader. I was going to call you next week or the week after."

Another time the writer met a woman he was drawn to, gave her his novel. "You don't have to like it," he said. "The book and the author aren't the same thing. Sometimes books you've done are like your high-school yearbook photo." Several days later he received a letter from her. "Your book touched me in a deep place," her letter began.

D<small>ISAGREEING</small> with the notion that making books and making babies are somehow similar, Flaubert argues that writing more closely resembles constructing a pyramid:

> There's some long-pondered plan, and then great blocks of stone are placed one on top of the other, and it's back-breaking, sweaty, time-consuming work. And all to no purpose! It just stands like that in the desert! But it towers over it prodigiously. Jackals piss at the base of it, and bourgeois clamber to the roof of it, etc. Continue this comparison.

✐ ✐ ✐

TWO years later, the writer tries to reconstruct an evening in Paris when he dined with a woman in her late forties, very tall and quite trim, silver hair cropped, enormous Spock ears exposed, dressed in sweater, black pants, and heels. Jean Seberg, Joan of Arc. "You're a writer," she said before the main course. "Would you like to hear my life story?" Dinner had started at ten, and he'd wandered the city most of the day, aperture perhaps too open. "Yes," he said. "Please."

Born, raised in Australia. Mother: many affairs with little attempt to hide them. Father: malformation of the penis, which apparently legitimized his wife's infidelities if not the manner in which they were conducted.

At 17, she went off to Europe to study music. Was followed by one of her mother's lovers, sent, she said, by the mother to seduce her. Which he did. Soon after, she met her future husband, a French baron. Though in his mid-twenties, he was a kind of sexual innocent. He courted her—apparently it took forever for him to try for a kiss—and finally won her hand. They moved to his château, raised two daughters. During her marriage she'd had only one affair, on-going for years, once a week, every week. Throughout her marriage she continued to give concerts, was finally gaining some real recognition as a pianist. Her husband had recently fallen in love—quite chastely, so far, as when he'd fallen in love with her—but was threatening divorce. He was also convinced, without cause, she thought, that he was in the final stage of a terminal illness.

Remembering this dinner, the writer regretted the long day preceding, the months of travel. He'd just been too tired to take the story in. What, for instance, was that malformation of the penis? She'd used a medical term. He was also dismayed to find he could recall few of her actual words, one exception being a bitter, "He knew nothing about women when we met; he had slept just with prostitutes."

The writer could remember with any certainty the wording of only one other phrase. Threatening to leave, her husband suggested she'd be unable to function without him. He told her, she said: "You cling to me like a limpet."

"Am I in the book?" she asked.
"No, kiddo, no," he replied. "Not unless you want to be."

*T*HE writer in early 1975, nearly thirty-one, second book finished, still improvising a life. Hauling out the battered trimaran up the Oakland Estuary, scraping rudder and hulls, applying copper bottom paint. Thinking about sailing somewhere. Possible detective work looming, investigating Watergate-related corporate wrongdoing. Possible stint in Volunteers for Africa. Doing the final draft of an introduction for a book of photographs about Berkeley. Not knowing if or when he'll want to write again, but contemplating a mystery novel, a book on African shore fishermen, stories about men and women in and out of love, or an account of following in the tracks of Cabeza de Vaca (the conquistador who left a record of his heroic trek across the southwest). Needing income, however, needing also another taste of the life he once thought he'd live, he takes on a three-month project for a foundation. The assignment: to look into violent crime by juveniles in New York City. Following a spate of murders by teenagers, there's been a wave of fear and anger. What if anything can the foundation do to help?

Work. The writer's colleagues are intelligent and motivated, the office relaxed, stipend more than fair. He moves around the city talking to experts, victims, administrators, reformers, judges, criminals. Hears descriptions of violence, broken homes, poverty, rotten schools, the absence of social services. How save the children? How save the public from them? Down to work each morning on the subway, in on Madison Avenue past the elevator controller and up twelve floors. A report to read, for instance, "The Delinquent Child: A Plethora of Problems." Call from a professor who argues that it costs $20,000 a year to incarcerate a juvenile (plus court costs, costs to the victim, and probable future costs of recidivism, welfare, etc.). Why not, then, spend almost any amount on prevention programs? Call from another professor, who argues there is no way to predict which children are prone to extreme violence.

New York. Blind man in the subway, sign saying, "It could be you." Woman at 79th and Columbus, no one near her, screaming, "Don't touch me." Elderly man in coat and tie outside Scribner's bookstore on Fifth Avenue, shouting—at the writer?—"How can you whistle when they crucified Jesus?" A young black woman laughing, saying, "Happy Easter."

On his way back to work, 42nd at Fifth. Comes the question, right in his face, "Are you Jewish?" Clearly from out of town, he says without thinking, "Yes," is instantly pulled into a Winnebago parked at the curb. Phylacteries hogtied around left arm and forehead / yarmulke slapped on pate / prayer incanted (*"Baruch atah . . ."*) / collection can for the Lubavitcher Hasids shoved into hand, and—poof!—the writer is back on 42nd Street, lapsed time perhaps twenty-three seconds. In the elevator at work several minutes later, a woman not only makes eye contact—taboo, taboo—but smiles. "One of us is wearing perfume," she says coyly. Manhattan is an island, the writer tells himself. What if the tunnels collapse, the bridges go down?

Work. Head filled with information. A kind of sexual energy in the task, all the motion, commotion, but almost no time for much of what is also real, the small, the latent, the backstage. For example, heading to a meeting the writer sees one of the secretaries Xeroxing her hand. "For my palmist," she explains brightly. "Oh," he says, and sits down in the conference room with a West Coast expert on child abuse around the country. Thirty thousand cases annually in New York City alone, the man says. Violence to children, violence from them. What else do we expect? Indeed. This kind of work may be something the foundation should support. Nonetheless, his attention flagging, the writer looks at the man more closely. Human enough, it seems. Suit and tie, college ring, gold wedding band. But what kind of person is he, really? And, one moment please, what's that thin, very thin, too-thin gold chain on his left wrist? Suddenly the writer realizes he's just been asked a direct question. "Do you mind repeating that?"

Cut off from dreams, reflections. Up at day's end to the Y on Central Park West, a quick scotch to relieve pressure on the pineal gland, then three miles around the reservoir by the Guggenheim Museum. Or, in bad weather, three miles—sixteen laps / mile—around the track inside. Hundreds of runners turning into butter. Box on the wall containing slips of paper with aphorisms, quotes. Take one, enter the flow.

The bounty of the city's insanities. An enormous fat woman in a restaurant in Little Italy singing bawdy songs, tambourine beating against her stomach, a very short old man, belt at sternum, by her side. The song's refrain something about dying with it in your hand, a black hunchback behind them on guitar. Or, in Central Park, a celebration of the end of the war in Vietnam, conga drums throbbing, much dope being smoked, the Dakota and nearby piles shimmering in the haze as if soon to levitate.

The writer's final report, and with it an invitation for him to stay on at the foundation. Eating a corned beef on light rye on the steps of the New York Public Library, he thinks it over. This is not only a good job but good works. He can feel the hormonal adjustment. Why not come in from the cold? He munches on his pickle, takes another swig of diet cola. Watches a wino nearby. Of course there's no hurry to get back to the office. Self-direction, good will are assumed. He studies the wino, finds himself trying to name the emotion the wino evokes. And then, just like that, up it comes: envy.

The sad truth is, the writer doesn't want to go back to the office. Age thirty, he wants to have nowhere to go. He wants to be the one to watch the days slide by, the one people hurry past, the one with time and space to take it all in. He wants this though, less pure a spirit than the wino, he'll no doubt feel the need to make something of what he's not doing. Something like a book, probably. Yes, something like a book. If, that is, the hormones can readjust. If the noise hasn't cracked a vital chromosome. If he can just get off of this crazy island.

EVERY once in a while the writer experiences a period during which ideas keep coming to mind. Though at the moment these ideas illuminate, in fact they are seldom exotic: the writer is simply perceiving the familiar in a slightly different way. Nonetheless, what was prosaic appears mysterious. Exhilarated, the writer makes notes. Later, when he works on a book, these notes both evoke the original thought and, occasionally, provoke fiction.

Often, settling in at his desk, the image of putting on a harness occurring to the writer, he again achieves a keen sense of the enormous distance between idea and story. Realizes once more that a story exists only in the telling.

*IN The Needs of Strangers*, Michael Ignatieff argues that "We need words to keep us human. Our needs are made of words: they come to us in speech, and they can die for lack of expression. . . . Without the light of language, we risk becoming strangers to our better shelves."

*Strangers to our better selves.* There are times when the writer, (temporarily?) estranged from reading and writing, begins to feel increasingly not himself. Diminished, that is. Less understanding of others, savoring less of the world around him. Meaner. In one such period, a partial image of his condition came to him: he was a creature lost in a forest. But what kind of creature? And what forest? The writer could not tell, except for his sense that the creature was without power of speech.

Subsequently, mood improving, again reading, again writing, he recalled this incomplete image, decided that perhaps the forest had been enchanted. That there was a love which had transformed and restored him. *Enchanted / transformed restored:* that there was a story to explain what had . . . *befallen* him, its very existence of course suggesting that he'd found his way home.

VIETNAMESE, born in Singapore, a translator of several oriental languages, her English is fluent but, to the writer's ear, sometimes slightly out of synch. For instance, responding sympathetically to a small problem he describes, she says, "A fine kettle of fish." Suddenly the whole language falls away from him. Is the phrase merely archaic? Is it her slight accent or the cadence of her words that give the phrase just enough spin to utterly confound him? Fishing for compliments, something fishy, large fish / small pond, neither fish nor fowl, other fish to fry, fisher of men: OK, OK. But is it not a fine kettle of something else, a fine something else of fish?

Later, as they undress, she says, "I want a man with a slow hand." Recognizing the line from the Pointer Sisters' hit, the writer mutters the chorus to himself as he takes off Adidas, socks, pants:

> I want a man with a slow hand
> I want a lover with an easy touch
> I want somebody who will
>     spend some time
> Not come and go in a heated rush

Turning back the covers, the writer wonders just what gives him pause. Is it merely that in this context appropriate use of the phrase requires an accompanying hint of irony? Thus again awakened to the mysteries of language, the writer finds himself more or less ready for bed.

On the rare occasion friends in California see the writer in coat and tie they express surprise. Out of character. Of course, they missed his college years, Oxbridge-on-Charles, jacket and tie mandatory for all meals. Many undergraduates left a sports coat and shirt with knotted tie on the rack outside the dining hall. Arriving at mealtime in jeans and T-shirt, they'd pull the partially buttoned shirt over the head and slip into the jacket while moving toward the serving line. Some student couturiers also cut the shirt off at the sternum, the better to avoid having to tuck it in.

Clothes. From childhood, the writer remembers a Babe Ruth baseball jacket. A Lone Ranger belt. An Eisenhower jacket, black flecked with reds, yellows, greens. The annual shipment of a wealthy uncle's used silk ties, massive, pyramidal, bib-like. Anomalous also because the children were discouraged from paying too much attention to appearance. Propriety, not vanity. Of course, cost was a consideration: things were quickly worn out, outgrown. Often the writer shopped at Sears or Robert Hall, hazardous because at, say, thirteen, six one / one hundred and thirty pounds, he had matchstick legs that disappeared in the ample cut of the men's chinos. Winter days were a particular misery, pants billowing like a spinnaker, gusts howling up and in from the cuffs. Fortunately, he acquired a fashion consultant in the form of the girl he began dating. She'd shop diligently at Filene's basement, returned once with a black cashmere overcoat the writer still wears. She also knitted sweaters, stations of the cross of her love, needles ever smaller as their relationship progressed.

By the time the writer started college he'd discovered corduroy Levis and workshirts, leather boots and / or sandals. Think of Pete Seeger, Steve McQueen, Richard Fariña, early Dylan. Of course he smoked Marlboros. By 1965, he'd become enamoured of suede (and had a pair of leather pants in which to ride the obligatory motorcycle). By 1966, seeing someone new, he'd phased in Marimekko shirts, a tie-dyed headband, black undershirts, and a strand of silver beads. He also went shopping for tooled leather boots and a sheepskin jacket.

Sartorially speaking, the seventies were a period of retrenchment for the writer. Though he continued to browse at Abercrombie and Fitch, generally he wore what he already owned, what was at hand, what could be machine washed. Thrift shop treasures, gear from yard sales. (Very heavy) hiking boots, Woolrich jackets. A watch cap. He kept his keys on a sail hank attached to a belt loop. Ranches, boats, writing: the rugged life, eased only by several Viyella shirts, a suede jacket, and a new pair of dress boots.

By 1980, teaching as a visiting writer, he'd often start class with a figure-modeling session, pulling in a passing student to sit as the group described each article of clothing and tried to infer something about character. "No one gets to go naked in this vale of tears," he told the class. What was the piece of clothing, what did wearing it suggest? In this context, in others.

One day, nobody out in the hall, the writer stood as the model. He was wearing a tweed coat purchased in London in 1961, Hush Puppies, a work shirt, and corduroys: freewheeling younger academic circa 1965. "And what about the belt?" the writer asked the class. He'd had it made years before up in Nevada City, in the foothills of the Sierras, had chosen the black leather and silver settings to evoke the Lone Ranger belt of his childhood. "Imitation silver," one student suggested, leaving the writer more than a little put out.

Of course, even what is freely chosen can confine. Recently he attended a gathering in Marin County. Doctors, computer people, lawyers, *nouvelle* restauranteurs, and academics on a Sunday afternoon, most males decked out in coats and slacks, shirts open at the collar, gold at the throat. He himself had elected the usual—Ferragamo boots, corduroy Levis *mit* neo-Lone Ranger belt, Viyella shirt, denim jacket. Thus attired, he mixed, mingled, snacked, asked people what they did, was asked, listened, responded. "A writer?" one fellow replied, looking him over a second time. "Right," the man then said, as if he should have known.

*T*HE January afternoon he finished his third book was high, clear, blue, the familiar interval between the orderly cycle of winter rainstorms. He'd been doing last revisions of a story, had also thought of adding another piece or two. But suddenly he realized there was nothing more he wanted to say, nor could he find a point of purchase for further editing. He was a little surprised, but there it was: between one moment and the next, without a sound, the book had passed out of his hands.

Not expecting the woman he lived with to return until she finished work, he decided to go to a local outdoor cafe. Nothing unusual here: while writing the book the last year and a half, often he'd take a short break, let himself unwind before digging in again. But always the book was central, the break only that, something to give him new energy for the central task. This time, however, after an hour he found himself still looking out at the bay. A scale model there before him: Golden Gate Bridge, Alcatraz, Angel Island, freighters moving slowly toward the Farrallones. Another hour passed. The woman at the next table finished reading a book on alternative therapies. Two lovers rendezvoused. An old man wrote a letter. Several high school kids talked about heavy metal. And still the writer stayed, surprised, pleased, by the amplitude of the day, all these lives.

More hours went by. Finally, sun setting out behind Mount Tamalpais, well north of west, the writer began to smile. Where had he been? How much he'd forgotten. And then he heard himself begin to laugh, to see the world so wide.

CONSIDER the case of nineteenth-century French writer Gérard de Nerval, fixed in popular memory as the poet who walked a lobster on a blue silk ribbon in the gardens of the Palais-Royal. According to Richard Holmes, even while saddled with debts Nerval lived out the "image of the insouciant, romantic traveller dashing off brilliant copy in distant lands between amorous assignations." Further, though drawn to solitude, Nerval had "very little psychological or emotional support for the kind of life he was trying to lead: no doting parents like Gautier's, no faithful wife like Murger's, no exotic lover like Baudelaire's, no attached sister like Wordsworth's." This at the moment when French society worshipped financial success even as it idealized the bohemian artist, a contradiction bound to trouble a doctor's son who'd squandered an inheritance.

Traveling in Egypt, Nerval found the ibis "nothing but a desert bird, the lotus a vulgar onion plant, and the Nile a murky red river with slate-grey reflections," concluded that by voyaging in search of the ideal he'd lost, "kingdom by kingdom, province by province, the most beautiful half of the universe, and soon I shall not know any more where to seek a refuge for my dreams." Suffering periods of madness, Nerval committed suicide at forty-five, both his art and his life exemplary, if in quite different ways.

THOUGH his books of short fiction allowed change of voice or characters as he wrote, permitted completion of something every month of two, his novel did not. And, the writer often reminded himself as he worked on it, he hadn't even intended a novel, saw nothing inherently higher or finer in the longer form, had simply found himself with an intriguing fragment which kept refusing narrow boundaries. Nonetheless, dog-paddling into the darkness, turning 38, turning 39, somewhere out in the middle of wherever, wondering—between periods of crazy exultation—if he'd like the novel when he finished, if he finished, it dawned on him that fiction was the wave of the past. Computers, video, journalism, this was what was real now. Several established writers in the area had novels no one wanted, a major publisher was going under, lists at many houses cut, editors fired. "Writers are like actors," a novelist told him at lunch one day, eyes twinkling. "Always waiting for a slap in the face."

In this period, he found himself reading biographies of writers. Though he needs to read almost as much as he needs to breathe, the writer can't stand the sight of other people's fiction when working on his own. Also, he's always loved biography, fiction posing as fact, savors the order redeemed from chaos, the bright-eyed presumption of coherence. Reading these biographies as he worked on his novel, however, he began to realize he was searching for something. Kindred spirits, perhaps? Clues to what his life had become?

The category "writers" is probably what Vonnegut describes as a "granfalloon," that is, an artificial union (like, say, a university or nation), as opposed to a "karass," an authentic bond (with the mugger who shoots you, for example). Nonetheless, four books behind him, into and lost in a fifth, having set out years before simply *to write*, during the next months he worked his way through biographies of Miller, Beckett, Stevenson,

Dinesen, Mailer, Lewis, Porter, Agee, Gissing, Sitwell, Corvo, Dostoevsky, Balzac, London, Stendhal, Hemingway, Woolf, Eliot, Rhys, Faulkner, Tolstoy, Conrad, Melville, Whitman, Fitzgerald. Crazily, the more he read the more he found himself like a prosecutor marshaling evidence against the genus. Miller dunning friends for money at age forty-five; Beckett riddled with psychosomatic cysts and boils; Whitman writing (and then quoting!) pseudonymous reviews of his own book; Tolstoy advising Chekhov not to waste his time writing plays.

What, you might ask, had he expected? Writers are human. Perhaps they would have been less attractive had they not written. Perhaps biographers seek the sensational lives. Perhaps these writers simply exhausted their virtues on the page. And so what? Against what standard was he measuring them? ("You know so many artists who are fools," a she says in one of Marianne Moore's poems. A he replies, "You know so many fools who are not artists.") Why couldn't he read these lives more sympathetically? What about Chekhov's extraordinary range of commitments, Wells's heroic refusal to be trapped as a draper's assistant? Wasn't Beckett brave in refusing again and again to yield to his parents' desire that he return to the family business? Wasn't Dinesen remarkable to insist on her own vision no matter how many times she failed? Yes, yes, yes—but his heart was moving toward a different conclusion.

Nor did it help when the writer came across this ferocious passage in Erich Auerbach's *Mimesis*:

> Documents of the kind represented by Flaubert's correspondence and the Goncourt diary are indeed admirable in the purity and incorruptibility of their artistic ethics, the wealth of impressions elaborated in them, and their refinements of sensory culture. At the same time, however, we sense . . . something oppressively close in these books. They are full of reality and intellect but poor in humor and inner poise. The purely literary, even on the highest level of artistic acumen . . . limits the power of judgment, reduces the wealth of life, and at the same time distorts the outlook upon the world of phenomena . . . what finally emerges,

despite all their intellectual culture and artistic incorruptibility, is a strangely petty total impression: that of an "upper bourgeois" egocentrically concerned over his aesthetic comfort, plagued by a thousand small vexations, nervous, obsessed by a mania—only in this case the mania is called "literature."

Finally, finally, he finished his novel, but even with the book out of his hands he wrestled with what it meant to write, to be a writer. One day he discussed Faulkner's life with his friend Peter, proprietor of a bookstore near his house. *Discussed?* Argued against. "Faulkner just played at being a country boy," the writer told his friend. "He was with Sherwood Anderson in New Orleans and then up to Greenwich Village by the time he was twenty-five. He faked a war wound, pretended to need a cane. He was a poseur." Seldom reluctant to speak his mind, Peter adjusted the bill of his Giants' baseball cap, said severely, "All that is irrelevant, meaningless."

Sound counsel, but still the writer couldn't let it go, though he was heartened when he considered the careers of Pynchon and Salinger. Pynchon, who seems to have absolutely no public life. And Salinger, who at the height of his game decided to stop publishing. There was also B. Traven, whoever he was. And di Lampedusa, *The Leopard* rejected during his lifetime, published posthumously.

In this period, the writer read a biography of William Saroyan. Probable anti-Semite, compulsive gambler, rotten father, lonely old man. Several weeks later, the writer picked up a copy of *My Name Is Aram*. "One day back there in the good old days when I was nine and the world was full of every imaginable kind of magnificence and life was still a delightful and mysterious dream. . . ." The writer laughed with pleasure. Young, strong, aware that it was alive, this voice was determined to sing. Oh, he could sense the book's limits in these lines. And he knew what the author would become. But then he thought of Grace Paley's "Conversation with My Father." And John Cheever's "Goodbye, My Brother." These two fine stories had more than once lifted his spirits, made him want to write. And then, smiling, he remembered the conclusion of *One Hundred Years of Solitude*. He'd been on his feet cheering those last thirty pages.

OK, the writer said to himself. OK. *The Executioner's Song. Out of Africa. In Our Time. Lord Jim. The Colossus of Maroussi. Torregreca. A Death in the Family. The Digger's Game. Henderson the Rain King. A River Runs Through It. Middlemarch. The Leopard. King Solomon's Mines. Narrow Road to the Deep North. The Book of Ebenezer LePage. Candy. The Kreutzer Sonata. A Woman Named Solitude. Mrs. Bridge. The Magician. The Dubliners. McTeague. The Milagro Beanfield War. The Peregrine. Great Expectations. Swann's Way. Moby Dick. A Fan's Notes. The First Circle. Wuthering Heights. The Baron in the Trees.* Books, books. Some larger, some finer, some truer, but all books that had pleased or taught him, books that had made him want to read, to continue to read. To write, to continue to write.

In this instant, it seemed clear that the writing itself was more than enough. And all the rest? Only the noise of the world, no more than also true. Right? Right? Well—yes. At least for the moment, he said to himself, acknowledging just how little it would take to make him suffer another change of heart.

IN *The Past Recaptured,* Proust writes:

> And then a new light, less dazzling, no doubt, than that other illumination which had made me perceive that the work of art was the sole means of rediscovering Lost Time, shone suddenly within me. And I understood that all these materials for a work of literature were simply my past life; I understood that they had come to me, in frivolous pleasures, in idleness, in affection, in unhappiness, and that I had laid them up in store without divining the purpose for which they were destined or even their continued existence any more than a seed does when it forms within itself a reserve of all the nutritious substances from which it will feed a plant. Like the seed, I should be able to die once the plant had developed. . . .

But as Paul Jay observes:

> Marcel "remembers" the past only as far as he forgets his actual past so as to create it imaginatively. . . . Loss, oblivion, isolation; these are the words that describe Marcel's relationship to his past. They posit memory not as the source of insight and renewal but as the point of departure leading toward their creation in the artist's own imagination. With this operation as the key to the efficacy of his autobiographical act, the text cannot, must not, avoid becoming a fictional history.

L<small>EAN</small>, wiry, in his early forties, a recording engineer, John runs four to eight slow miles every evening. Occasionally, the writer sees him at the track at sunset, shares a few laps with him. John is always almost insistently amiable, a good raconteur, quick with advice about running gear, warmup techniques, health care. He ran competitively in college, he says, seems to know what he's talking about.

One evening, waving across the infield at a woman who's heading to her car, John tells the writer that he meets most of the women he dates at the track, that he sleeps with several new women every week.

"Every week? Jesus."

"You think I'm lying?"

"No, no."

"You think it's wrong?"

"Wrong? Oh, I don't know. Compulsive, maybe."

"Well if that's all, then what was the surprise in your voice?"

"You mean, beyond awe at the sheer numbers involved?"

"Yes."

"I don't know, I guess I was marveling at the idea of having to tell a story about yourself that frequently. I mean, if I really think about it, you must say something before going to bed. I suppose I was wondering abut having to hear your own voice doing it over and over and over like that."

"You know, it's interesting you should say that," John replies. "Very interesting. To tell you the truth, I really enjoy figuring out what they want to hear. In some ways, it's the part I like best."

S*TRATEGY,* tactics. How to keep moving forward on the manuscript. Writing new material, rewriting, doing stenography, shifting the level of demand. Retyping a story, sometimes, to pick up physical momentum. Retyping a story, sometimes, to mime writing and so recall how to approach the thing itself.

❦ ❦ ❦

ONE evening, reading an interview with Edna O'Brien, the writer learned that after her mother died she'd found a copy of *The Country Girl* "buried under pillows and bolsters in the drawer. The dedication page had been torn out and the offending words inked over throughout the book. I realized my mother was ashamed."

That night, late, the writer woke thinking of the period just after publication of his first book. One afternoon he stopped by his father's office at the hospital, perhaps to give him a lift home. This was in 1972, not more than a year before his father died. The writer would have been twenty-seven. Wearing a white lab coat as always, his father was thinner than ever, carefully cajoling his system into functioning for another day of work. Dreams to make real—a new hospital to complete—he had no impulse to prolong his life by semi-invalidism. Though the writer's father seemed proud his son had published a book—of course he respected accomplishment, and the reviews had been favorable—he was disturbed by the book's content. Too much danger, danger that had nearly swallowed his son whole. Back in the early sixties when the anti-war movement was getting started, during one of what the writer and his siblings called "summit conferences," his father warned him about agents provocateurs. Term so dated, the writer had to fight not to laugh. Eighteen years old, he indulged his old man.

The book must also have seemed uncomfortably confessional to his father. His mother wrote, of course, but her verse was too elliptical for easily mined revelations. His father had spent his adult life in academic medicine in Boston, had a European sense of decorum. In the book so much was sad or seedy. Did one really need to talk about such things?

Though he never said so, his message seemed to be "Well done, son, but now what?" He'd been scrupulous not to pressure his children into medicine, but finally, perhaps because he was dying, seemed to fear he might have protected them too well. As professor and physician he'd taught, healed, done research, administered, shaped public policy and still endured periods of professional difficulty. How would writing function as a career? What was the virtue in jeopardy, absent some statement from his son that writing was his heart's desire? And perhaps he'd simply spent too much time with dying children to believe that stories were enough for a man to create in the world. And yet—for the writer, his parents' lack of regard for wealth, their freedom from many kinds of received wisdom, his mother's careers in the arts, all of this enabled him to go his own way.

Daybreak not far off late that night, still the writer continued too think it over. I suppose, he finally said to himself, I suppose that if I had a child as headstrong, as dazzlingly ignorant, and as fearless as I was and that child wanted to be a writer . . . Well, of course all of it would be different. Still, I suppose I'd probably try to impel him or her in another direction. In this I seem to be my father's son. Not that anything Daddy did or didn't say could have stopped me. Or any such child.

A*RE* you published?
What's the title?
Never heard of it.
Can you . . . do you . . . make a living at it?

"*I* NEVER thought I would write a book," kidnapped heiress Patty Hearst writes in her autobiography, "and probably wouldn't have were I not constantly asked, 'When are you going to talk about what happened to you?' The question arises so often that I finally decided to address it once and for all and tell the complete story. . . ."

*Once and for all. The complete story. To talk about what happened.* By the time the book appeared, Hearst, 27, was surely no novice at storytelling. Just after being abducted, she received a lesson in diction from the Symbionese Liberation Army. Blindfolded, hands tied, she told her captors she needed to go to the bathroom. The voices "all screamed with laughter; something was enormously funny. . . ." She did not get the joke until one of the voices said, "Listen, if you gotta go, say, I gotta go pee. . . . That's the way poor people talk." Then, the third day in the closet that was her cell, General Field Marshal Cinque Mtume (a.k.a. Donald DeFreeze) started what he called interrogations. Weeks later, Hearst tells us, Cinque gave her the option of joining the SLA. Saying she believed that her only chance to live was to convince the group she'd converted, "I poured my heart out to them, pleading to be allowed to join them in the revolution that would free the poor and oppressed people from the fascist corporate military state. . . . The more blatant and preposterous my statements became, the more they believed them."

When, finally, Hearst was captured by the FBI, she of course had to explain to family and lawyers what had transpired since her abduction and apparent conversion. "Little did I know then," she writes, "that that would be only the first of many times I would have to try to tell what happened. . . ." Subsequently, she presented her story to psychiatrists, and, through her lawyer, swore to the veracity of carefully chosen excerpts.

Finally, in an effort to win a pardon she told her story to journalists.

In a television interview after publication of her book, asked by Barbara Walters how she planned to explain her life with the SLA to her daughter, Hearst replied, "Maybe I won't tell her anything. Maybe I'll just let her hear about it from friends, like sex or something." Then she laughed. A little surprised by what she'd said, perhaps, or tired of Walter's treacly solicitousness. Nonetheless, there seemed little chance Hearst would let anything just happen in terms of her story: more likely, she'd tell it for some time to come. Thus she'd integrate the dazzlingly disparate lives she'd led while making as sure as possible that the story would (continue to) have a happy ending.

THE poet and the writer at lunch, waiter periodically administering California cuisine.

"Remember my friend Philip?" the writer asks. "Lives in Mill Valley? He just told his wife he's going to have an affair."

"That he's *going* to have an affair?"

"She called me, said, 'You're his friend. I just want to ask what in the name of male menopause my husband is up to.' She was bullshit. Anyway, I don't have the slightest idea why Philip's doing this. He loves his wife, likes her, too, has always been good to her. In the meantime she blames me."

"You? Why?"

"The woman he's telling his wife he's going to have an affair with is an old friend of mine. Philip, this woman, and I had lunch together one day in North Beach. It was a beautiful afternoon. I had to take off right after we ate, but they were thinking about a walk to Marina Green. 'Why didn't you go with them?' his wife asked me. She was really pissed."

"Who wouldn't be?" the poet replies, leaning back as the waiter sets down the coffee.

"Really." The writer studied his companion for a moment. "So why the long face?"

"That story."

"What about it?"

"Shit, here we are, past forty, and this kind of thing keeps happening."

"Poet, make my day. Perhaps you should head for the desert, choose the most comfortable pillar. Otherwise, this is what we—we prose writers, anyway—have been given by the gods to describe, appraise, celebrate."

"Celebrate? What's to celebrate in this story?"

"Well, we're alive to tell it, for one thing. Then too, we have how we tell it. Right? Meanwhile, we still have to figure out what the story is. Maybe everything will work out between them. Maybe it's for the best that it doesn't. It's just too soon to tell. Until that time, why not console yourself by thinking how much worse it could be."

"For instance."

"Well, consider my friend Jack, whose wife's currently actually having an affair. For openers, be so kind as to ask me how he learned this."

"She told him?"

"A very honest woman. But that's not the bad part. The bad part is that his wife's seeing—you'll pardon my use of the verb—a blind guy."

"Jesus. Not fair."

"Jack's sentiments exactly. He also said, 'How in the name of all that's holy can I compete with a blind guy?'"

"How can he? What did you tell him?"

"I told him to gouge his eyes out."

"No, really."

"Really? Well, Jack said to me, 'You're a writer, you must have learned something all these years while decent people were out making an honest living.'"

"How did you respond to that?"

"I told him I'm a writer, not a therapist. Then I told him to see you. I said poets must know something useful. Orpheus, Tiresias. Eternal verities, entrail reading, etc., etc."

"Come on. What did you say?"

"Well, first I told him I didn't think he should gouge his eyes out. Then I said, 'Jack, my friend, in truth you have no cause for concern. The fact of the matter is, your wife's sightless lover has absolutely nothing on you.' 'How can you say that?,' he asked me, 'how can you stand there and say that?' 'Because, Jack,' I told him, 'for you not to see what was going on between them all these months, that compels any impartial observer to conclude you are either a saint or . . .'"

". . . blind as a bat."

"Close, Mr. Poet. I believe my actual words were, 'Blind as a fucking bat.'"

"All the difference in the world."

"Really, though I don't know that Jack would have thought so."

MARASMUS: progressive emaciation, a wasting away, gradual loss of strength not caused by some actual disease. Now reversible in hospitalized infants, apparently, simply by the grace of sufficient physical contact.

Which brings to mind this passage from Philip Roth's *The Anatomy Lesson*:

> He thought he had chosen life but what he had chosen was the next page. Stealing time to write stories, he never thought to wonder what time might be stealing from. Only gradually did the perfecting of a writer's iron will begin to feel like the evasion of experience, and the means to imaginative release . . . like the sternest form of incarceration. He thought he'd chosen the intensification of everything and he'd chosen monasticism and retreat instead.

Or these words written by fifty-seven-year-old bachelor Henry James:

> This loneliness, what is it still but the deepest thing about one? Deeper about *me*, at any rate, than anything else: deeper than my "genius," deeper than my "discipline," deeper than my pride, deeper, above all, than the deep countermining of art.

Or a press release about Jacqueline Susann's "full, never-before-revealed" life story, told at long last by her husband and co-author:

> While Miss Susann wrote her books all by herself, it was Irving Mansfield, her life's mate and inseparable companion, who helped her rewrite the publishing record books.

*Sternest form of incarceration. Deep countermining of art. All by herself.* Oh, isn't fiction a lonely game?

*T*ABLE cleared, they read their fortune cookies. "Books do not lead men astray," hers reads, and they laugh. His says, "An emptiness will soon be filled." But probably not tonight, he acknowledges to himself. Through dinner she's been talking about how coercive language is. "Think about it," she tells the writer. "If you say 'I love you' to someone, it's a kind of argument. What you're also saying is, 'Therefore you should love me.'" She looks at the writer appraisingly, both of them increasingly self-conscious. "Don't you see," she says, "language is dangerous." He nods: any more of this, he'll be a believer.

In 1964, just twenty, the writer drove out to California from Boston for the first time, he and one of his college roommates heading west for summer jobs. On the fourth night they stopped at a ranch in Wyoming. "About how far is it from here to San Francisco?" the writer asked the rancher the next morning. He'd been sitting on the top rail of the corral, feeling photogenic. "Oh, heck, maybe a thousand miles," the rancher responded. "But don't worry. It's all downhill." Given the rancher's straight face and lack of affect in his voice, the writer was unsure whether he somehow believed this, or, Rockies and Sierras looming, intended figurative language.

In 1966, returning to California, the writer commenced what proved to be a sustained (and sustaining?) schizophrenia, an effort to span an ever more distant past and a present he was only partially equipped to accept as real. His early stories were something like letters home, descriptions of what he thought he'd found rendered in the tongue of the world he'd grown up in. Were, also, arguments with those he'd left behind—and that part of himself—about what was valid, acceptable. As he might have known, the past as he construed it stayed right with him, if only because he was too far from his origins to take them for granted.

This bicoastalitis, as the writer came to call it, had various effects, among them that for more than ten years he was the fellow who goes out to Oakland Coliseum to see the Athletics when the Red Sox are playing. When, that is, Boston comes to town. Sipping his beer, thinking of Fenway Park in Boston, a mile from where he grew up, the writer would ask those around him where they came from. Blessed with the unthinking specificity of true parochialism, they almost never said "Massachusetts" or "Boston" or "near Boston." No, it was "Roslindale" / "Metheun" / "Malden" / "Brighton" / "Watertown" / "Auburndale." Nor did most consider themselves exiles.

They'd left behind bitter cold, snowblowers, cars buried in drifts, dead batteries, the wind chill factor. Measuring California in meterological terms, they had no cause for nostalgia.

Weather notwithstanding, even if he had dispossessed himself, the writer found the differences hard to reconcile. One of his more explicit efforts at self-integration took the form of a book column for a local magazine. In an early piece he discussed Kevin Starr's *Americans and the California Dream*, responding particularly to Starr's portrait of Richard Henry Dana, Jr., author of *Two Years Before the Mast*. A neurasthenic Harvard undergraduate in the 1830s, Dana broke free by shipping out as a sailor, then spending more than a year on the West Coast. Much as California healed him, however, it inspired unease. Would he end up a beach bum, a common seaman? Back in Boston, after several years a lawyer married to a religious hypochondriac, Dana apparently would periodically don sailor's togs, go to a prostitute's room, administer a moral lecture, and then return home to inform his wife of his mission of mercy.

Starr also appraises the impact of the Donner party on nineteenth-century Californians. As he points out, after an erroneous short cut, "Families refused to look after the children of others—then refused water to children not their own." A man was killed, another abandoned. Then the snow trapped them in the Sierras. Following the rescue of the last of the survivors, contemporaries found in both their suffering and their cannibalism a symbol of communal failure, a metaphor for California as dystopia.

In addition, historian Starr presents an unsparing portrait of Jack London nearing the end of his life: obese, drunk, self-deceived, and, at last, a suicide. For both London and California, Starr argues, the problem was being intimidated by an East Coast that seemed "sophisticated, impervious, assured of its history, assured of its caste. [London's] flight into narcissm and fantasy . . . paralleled California's appropriation of a fabled Hispanic era and a mythically redemptive frontier."

Richard Henry Dana; Jack London; the Donner party: easterners coming west; westerners creating an image of themselves. Part of the writer's effort to measure the California he kept (almost) making his home in the language, and, to some degree, by the mores of the world he'd left behind. Eager also to convey irony's saving grace in a land of so many true believers, he reviewed a how-to book on levitation, and, fearing the imminent triumph of self-improvement, argued that breathing, for example, is not quite the same as breath therapy.

In a different forum in that same period—a syndicated radio program originating on the East Coast—the writer adopted a different persona, playing the stage Californian, in one piece arguing with pundits who suggested after the mass suicides at Jonestown that Reverend Jones could only have flourished in California. What, the writer asked, what of a cult that could send fifty thousand young men to die in southeast Asia? And as for Jones's reputation in history, perhaps his great mistake had been in not declaring Jonestown a nation. Making himself, for instance, its secretary of state, given the esteem someone like Henry Kissinger still enjoyed in Washington.

Shock value aside, part of what was at stake for the writer in these columns and radio pieces, as well as in his internal dialogue about choice of place to live, was his voice as a writer. Where he was coming from, so to speak. In California, he felt he had the freedom both to invent himself and to choose what seemed real—was, for example, impervious to displays of status which elsewhere might have inflicted a fatal dose of relative deprivation. Felt free, also, to err, be unreasonable, to settle for a partial truth. Again and again, in any case, the writer found himself acting as though if he went home he'd be someone else, that he would lose his mana, the force of vision he'd been granted by dispossessing himself.

In this period the writer received a call from an author who wanted his novel reviewed. Explaining that current fiction generally wouldn't function as the point of departure for his pieces, the writer suggested that the book be sent on to the magazine's other columnist. Undeterred, the author restated his request. When, finally, the writer intimated that their conversation should end, the author threatened his life. Though the man later phoned to apologize, the writer reproached himself: he'd drifted too far into what Flaubert, bachelor wistfully watching perambulators wheel by, referred to as "le vrai." Over and again the writer had learned that to write stories meant to decline certain opportunities. Instead of duking it out with a man determined to share his gift with unwilling others—O, Art in America!—it was time to again immerse himself in the truly destructive element. To resume the deep diving that is fiction. To endeavor, as Kafka suggested, to transform the I-madness into he-madness. Perhaps in that process alone would the writer find where he really lived. And thus, according to the odd calculus of his unconscious, discover who he really was.

WE find the mates we need, they say. We know what we're choosing. Well, over the course of eight years, a period in which the writer was more than once tempted to come in from the cold, this is some of what she brought to him:
- a hunger to live outside society, quietly, simply;
- an impulse toward wild places, for hawks / fogs / stars / strands / snow;
- a lack of fear of poverty;
- a passion for stories, above all stories of noble animals, or of humans in a state of grace;
- a root belief that though art is vital, of course not all art is vital;
- love, though she almost never used the word.

THE writer came late to Kafka, having avoided his work the way people avoid, say, the sight of blood. Perhaps too the writer resisted the current tendency to equate talent and pathology. As Richard Ellman points out, the prevailing paradigm of the artist is not Chaucer, diplomat and courtier, but Kafka, tubercular neurasthenic trapped in a losing oedipal struggle, a man trebly an outsider as a non-observant German-speaking Jew in Prague.

Warming up with Canetti's essay on Kafka's letters to Felice, the writer then read Ernst Pawel's biography. For Pawel, Kafka was in fact tortured, ambivalent, obsessed with shame and humiliation, someone who earned the right to say of himself, "I am a memory come alive." Nonetheless, Pawel argues, for all his self-loathing Kafka was also an effective career bureaucrat, a good athlete, did finally leave his parents' home, inspired remarkable loyalty in his friends, was not only attractive to women but capable of love. As for writing, Kafka's "ax to break the frozen sea within," Pawel concludes that it both justified Kafka's life and justified his not living it. Of course Kafka knew this: writing was not only a "form of prayer" but a "reward for serving the devil." Yet whatever the costs of such a calling and however nightmarish the vision, the very existence of Kafka's fiction testifies to a remarkable vitality.

Finishing the Pawel biography, thus grounded—inoculated?—the writer arrived at "A Hunger Artist." He'd just driven home from shopping that late spring day, had pulled up to the curb, radio playing, singing along with a country-and-western tune: "If the phone doesn't ring, it's just me." "A Hunger Artist" was written in 1922, when Kafka was forty, and begins, "During these last decades the interest in professional fasting has markedly diminished." As this deadpan premise is played out—one can almost see the author's sardonic smile, hear him saying "You're it" as he runs off—the story describes how, metier no longer in fashion, the once-famous hunger artist winds up in a circus cage. Forgotten, no one even keeping track of how long he's gone without food, the dying man begs the overseer's forgiveness because, he whispers, his fasting was nothing to admire. Rather, he fasted because "I couldn't find the food I liked. If I had, believe me, I should have made no fuss and stuffed myself like you or anyone else." With the hunger artist's death the cage is cleared, a young panther installed. "Even the most insensitive felt it refreshing to see this wild creature leaping around the cage that had so long been dreary."

Sun bright, plum and cherry in full bloom, the writer put the story down with a sense of having finished it less well off than the author, who'd at least experienced the satisfaction of giving form to something so disquieting. Not to mention the pleasure of anticipating its effect on others. Jesus, Kafka, the writer said to himself, you wrote it, it's yours. But of course now it was his too. All right, Kafka, he thought. Who wouldn't rather be the panther, eating without hesitation, joy of life "streaming from his throat." And even though "Fasting would surely come into fashion again . . . ," who in his right mind would want to identify with the hunger artist? Surely not a writer in California on a warm spring day, life eternal, happiness guaranteed. No. No way. It would take someone like a doomed Jew foolishly born into a Czech city late in the nineteenth century, blood libel and pogroms still in the air, death camps soon to follow. The latter a fate Kafka avoided because disease had its own more insistent agenda. He expired at forty-one from tuberculosis of the larynx, finally "quite unable to eat . . . dying of starvation and immersed in the galley proofs of *A Hunger Artist.*"

"You know that story in your book about the guy who watches his wife dancing with other men?" The male voice on the phone said it was calling long distance, from Washington, D.C., that mutual friends had provided the writer's number. "Well, what I wanted to know was, who told you?"

"Who told me what?"

"The story."

"No one told me the story. I didn't base it on something that happened to anyone else or to me. I wrote it, I made it up. You could even say I was exploring a possibility that might some day lead me to action, trying it on for size. But as far as I know that's the only connection the story has to the real world.

"Sure, I know, libel, you have to say that."

"No, really, I'm telling you truth as clearly as I can."

"O.K., O.K., don't get uptight, just answer me one more question. Was it my wife who told you?"

According to Mario Vargas Llosa, the Spanish inquisitors banned all fiction—the entire genre—from their American colonies; for 300 years, Hispano-Americans could read only contraband works of fiction. Though he once ridiculed the inquisitors, Llosa says, he came to believe that they in fact read fiction correctly. Auden, however, would have disagreed. As he wrote in response to Yeats's death, "Ireland has her madness and her weather still / For poetry makes nothing happen." According to Arthur Danto, Auden argued that "the political history of the world would have been the same if not a poem had been written, nor a picture painted, nor a bar of music composed."\*

Auden notwithstanding, the notion that fiction is inherently and / or effectively subversive will no doubt console those writers who subscribe to Susan Sontag's sense of "literature as privacy—as a social contribution, if you will, but only because the writer knows how to distance himself or herself from the collective din. . . ." Distance: the writer's capacity / obligation / need to stand back, stand off to the side. To make use of, describe, record, witness. Of the actors playing Hamlet, Lear, Ophelia, and Cordelia, Yeats wrote: "If worthy their prominent part in the play," they "Do not break up their lines to weep."

But of course there are always those who want more from the writer, who are, as Yeats wrote, "sick of the palette and fiddle-bow, / Of poets that are always gay. . . ." Nor will such people fail to be galled by the writer's truculence. "I never

---

\* Though Danto points out that it is of course difficult to appraise so empirical a claim, he says, speaking of Picasso's *Guernica*, that "even works intended to prick consciousness to political concern have tended by and large to provoke at best an admiration for themselves and a moral self-admiration for those who admired them."

really warmed / to the reformer or reformed," Frost wrote. And, in a letter, said:

> You wish the world better than it is, more poetical. . . . I wouldn't give a cent to see the world, the United States, or even New York made better. I want them left just as they are for me to make poetical on paper. I don't ask anything done to them that I won't do to them myself. I'm a mere selfish artist most of the time. The grief will be if I can't transmute it into poems. . . . My whole anxiety is for myself as a performer. Am I any good? That's what I'd like to know and all I need to know.

If Frost seems to revel in a protestation of ruthlessness, consider Rilke's vision:

> To want to improve the situation of another human being presupposes an insight into his circumstances such as not even a poet has toward a character he himself has created. How much less insight is there in the so infinitely excluded helper, whose scatteredness becomes complete with his gift. Wanting to change or improve someone's situation means offering him, in exchange for difficulties in which he is practiced and experienced, other difficulties that will find him perhaps even more bewildered. If at any time I was able to pour out into the mold of my heart the imaginary voices of the dwarf or beggar, the metal of this cast was not obtained from any wish that the dwarf or the beggar might have a less difficult time. On the contrary: only through a praising of their incomparable fate could the poet, with his full attention suddenly given to them, be true and fundamental, and there is nothing that he would have to fear and refuse so much as a corrected world in which the dwarfs are stretched out and the beggars enriched. The God of completeness sees to it that these varieties do not cease, and it would be a most superficial attitude to consider the poet's joy in this suffering multiplicity as an esthetic pretense.

From such sanguine lack of regret—and such presumption, the poet granting himself more insight than "the so infinitely excluded helper"—Nadine Gordimer would most vehemently demur:

> The creative act is not pure. . . . The writer is *held responsible;* and the verbal phrase is ominously accurate, for the writer not only has laid upon him responsibility for various interpretations of the consequences of his work, he is "held" before he begins by the claims of different concepts of morality—artistic, linguistic, ideological, national, political, religious—asserted upon him. He learns that his creative act was not pure even while being formed in his brain: already it carried congenital responsibility for what he represented in genetic, environmental, social, and economic terms when he was born of his parents.

Compelling, this view, but perhaps still somewhat abstract. For example, even as Nabokov argues that he doesn't "give a damn for the group, the community, the masses, and so forth," he nonetheless offers a set of political guidelines:

> Freedom of speech, freedom of thought, freedom of art. . . . Portraits of the head of the government should not exceed a postage stamp in size. No torture and no executions. No music, except coming through earphones, or played in theatres.

Clever, Nabokov's program, yet also perhaps not quite sufficient. But what kind of formula, then, can guide? Something like Flaubert's notion, that a writer should "wade into life as into the sea, but only up to the navel"? Or Solzhenitsyn's rule of thumb: the wolfhound is right, but the cannibal is wrong.

PACING. Writing a book of fiction is more marathon than sprint. Steady work, keeping the book the central obligation. Sustain.

And still—urgency, desperation. To create this cluster of lives, the rival and prior world asked for time / health / applause. For freedom from the laws of gravity.

*Tohu vavohu:* the nothingness out of which God made the firmament. The writer's blank page. Making love out of nothing at all.

THROUGH completion of his third book—he was thirty-three by then—he'd met perhaps five writers, knew only two of them well, one of them his mother. (It was surely convenient, his unexamined but heartfelt notion that as a poet she was in a different line of work.) For years he avoided writers, in part to spare himself any feeling of competitiveness. "You must live in quite a literary community," his editor said in 1975. Well, his neighbors were aliterate, wondered why he wanted quiet, were disturbed by his typing. On the other hand, part of no clique or school, he was free to find his way. Or to flounder.

Later, later, still another book behind him, he came to know a number of writers well, and, in time, to count several among his closest friends. One, with whom he fell in love, was from the start defined for him by their long-distance exchange of cards, letters, phone calls. So intelligible did she become to him through these words, so truly apprehended did he feel, that, suddenly, she was kin. She also gave him this gift: to remind him, in the exotic tongue of their tribe of two, just how much he loved language. With her—the array of words they drew on together, the new taste of even the most familiar phrases—he sometimes felt that at last he'd discovered his true idiom. Was, it almost seemed, speaking for the very first time.

∠ ∠ ∠

*E*ARLY 1970. Only recently in the vanguard, the revolutionary finds himself with a pregnant wife and no marketable skills. Desperate, he enrolls in a cram course for the California real estate broker's exam. Walking around campus one day, he beholds a room full of non-correcting IBM Selectrics, no humans in sight. Utterly forgetting his future as breadwinner and provider, perhaps involuntarily again catapulted to the understanding that there can be no such thing as private property, he picks up the machine, grunts—it is only technically a portable—and lugs it away. Selectric then sitting unused in his living room, the revolutionary bestows it on his friend the writer.

Over the ensuing fifteen years, the writer, a latent Luddite, resists the advent of more advanced machines, comes to think of himself as a simple man holding on to traditional values, in part because there are lots of used Selectrics around, like old VW bugs. Also, the Selectric seems to him an appropriate tool. Electric, yes, but he was born into a world with plugs, bulbs, ohms, is conversant with representations of such technology even if—*pace Zen and the Art of Motorcycle Maintenance*—he has no idea how it works. Further, the writer appreciates the quiet of the Selectric's revolving type ball, the machine's great innovation. Finally, if the medium is the message, the Selectric and Xerox both defined and articulated his *weltanschauung* as he reached manhood.

Over the years, meanwhile, the writer increasingly embraces the idea that clean copy objectifies the text, makes it easier to critique. Worse, he believes that even apparently rote retyping leads to rewriting. As time passes, however, he begins to feel that much of such retyping is in fact mere drudgery, this as his hunger for clean copy only increases. In the face of the many kinds of delayed gratification books require, he finds losing the capacity to live without a simulacrum of the page.

Early 1986: converted by the rhapsodies of friends and family, he purchases a computer, and, after several days of buyer's remorse, finds himself—happy. At last he can edit at will, can always print up another immaculate draft. Also alluring is the computer's capacity to compress. Small is indeed beautiful, he feels, a sentiment consonant with his impulse to explore the mysteries of the wide world within the limits of the page.

Two A.M. Waking up with an idea, the writer's switched on the computer. For a moment, yawning, he thinks of the Selectric upstairs in the closet. "Don't look back," the writer says to himself. Bob Dylan. "Don't look back?" Dylan had to be kidding.

Keys clicking, he begins to write, hears the contrapuntal movement of information from one disk to another, the exchange to his ear a kind of conversation. As if underwater, he thinks. Between, perhaps, two very large and quite benign cetaceans. Mother and child, possibly? A question he entertains only a moment before writing on into the night.

*THE* writer's mother, her mandarin approach to poetry. She published many books, but without a powerful older poet leading the way, without lecture tours, without a bureaucratic base from which to trade favors, without taking up timely strategies—the poet as guru, for instance, or the writer as victim. On the other hand, in her first career, as singer and actress, she tasted perhaps enough applause for a lifetime. And then she had four children, a strong marriage, financial stability through her husband's academic income. For her, poetry as a primary commitment began in her late thirties, and, though fierce in her hunger to write, she did little more to advance a career than send the poems out, a postal scale, envelopes of all sizes, and rolls of stamps in the closet. Of course she wanted an audience, but counted on the merits of her work to create it, an arguable proposition. Despite her many books, she never had any certainty that a given manuscript would be published, left a number of finished texts that found no taker. Nonetheless, in large part this was her choice, inasmuch as any of us are free to choose. She could always have administered grants, reviewed, run a press, taken a university position, done a newspaper column or radio show, hosted writing workshops, moved closer to New York, moved farther from New York— these various royal roads to advancement of a twentieth-century literary career.

   Thinking in this way about his mother's life as a poet, it dawned on the writer that at thirty-three he was not married, was not financially secure, had had no children, no other career. What, then, was he doing, to think that writing books was all it would take? To be so partially following in his mother's footsteps.

TWENTY years ago, writing a piece a week for the *Express Times*, the writer often called his friend Terry late at night to read what he'd just finished. Usually asleep when he phoned, she'd rouse herself, listen, say "That's good," and go back to bed. Within several days the paper would be out. If the writer went down to Telegraph Avenue to the Cafe Mediterraneum, friends and acquaintenances there would be reading his story.

Since then, the interval between finished work and public response has been considerably longer. Writing books, the writer has tried to have at least a nearly finished manuscript before signing a contract—before, that is, showing it to agent or editor. He's done this in part from an aversion to presenting work less good than it will be. Also, he's loath to ask others to imagine what is not on the page. Further, to contract for a book before completion seems to move it into the realm of obligation. Though publication is one of the writer's goals, the book receives life in the domain of dreaming, risk-taking, folly, the anti-social. True, the book's fate may include a corporation in lower Manhattan, graphic designer / sales conference / copy editor / jacket photo / press release. Still, the requisite freedom seems to be able to take forever with the book, or to abandon it.

While at work, however, the writer not surprisingly craves feedback. Occasionally, still, he calls his friend Terry (though no longer after ten P.M.), reads her some pages. Or asks a friend who stops by to read a story. In the living room. No text going out of the house, the writer thus controlling the terrain on which the manuscript is encountered. Doing this, the writer seeks to have some taste of the response he hopes the book will one day find, but without any desire for even helpful criticism. To begin with, the writer generally feels he knows what he's doing, or that he'll find out if he's patient. Further, manuscript pages, lacking the authority of a published book, are just too easy to find fault with, seem to invite collaboration.

Once, having sent off his novel to his agent, the writer headed up to ranch country. He'd worked on the book two years, was just beginning to take stock both of the book and of the life that had been so determined to produce it. On his arrival in Oregon, an old friend kept asking to read the manuscript. Despite reminding himself that of course the book was far more important to him that it could be to his friend, the writer finally said yes. Perhaps it was simply time to let the book begin its public incarnation.

To make a long story short, the friend didn't much like it. So there they were, out in the middle of nowhere, friend thinking he had to let the writer down gently. A moment made even less comfortable when the writer explained that while of course he'd prefer that his friend like the book, for him not to had to be at best irrelevant. Were his reading instrumental—were he, say, an editor or a powerful reviewer—it might have some practical significance. But even so, the writer simply could not allow any reader's criticism—or praise, for that matter—to shape his root opinion of the book. It sounded obdurate, he knew, only a step short of psychosis, but at some point blind trust was absolutely essential. Otherwise, really, how could he spend all that time in his study—how could one write at all?

SPEAKING of the artist, Tanner says in Shaw's *Man and Superman:*

> To women he is half vivisector, half vampire. He gets into intimate relations with them to study them, to strip the mask of convention from them, to surprise their inmost secrets, knowing that they have the power to rouse his deepest creative energies, to rescue him from cold reason, to make him see visions and dream dreams, to inspire him, as he calls it. . . .\*

Of his own marriage, which lasted just a year, Rilke wrote: "What was my house, then, except a foreign thing for which I had to work, what more my family than visitors who refused to leave?" Over and again Rilke sought love only to find himself unable to reconcile it with his vocation. Claiming to be "only a voice," he repeatedly implored those he had encouraged to love him to "love my solitude." Never able to believe that art was compatible with the demands of life, he felt that in reciprocating love the real function of the creative act would be lost.

Though author Evan Connell's view is more explicitly practical—he once said he avoided marriage lest with wife and children he end up bagging groceries—a writer's impulse to stay single may have at least as much to do with how one gets to tell one's tale. That is, beyond solitude's cool clarity and the self-dramatizing it both necessitates and sustains, there is no spouse or child to offer a competing version of stories—of self.

---

\* Not, of course, that such an artist need be male. "I am more interested in human beings than in writing," Anaïs Nin wrote, "more interested in love-making than in writing, more interested in living than in writing. More interested in becoming a work of art than in creating one. I am more interesting than what I write."

Further, like most people who live alone, away from his study the single writer is perennially a storyteller: others are apt to share at most a small portion of his life; there is always much to be filled in. The single writer then forever protagonist in his own drama, the wide world forever audience. Each anecdote—told, retold, worked, reworked—being readied for person or page.

E VERY year or so, the writer makes a point of leafing through his books. In search of the wellspring of his voice, perhaps, or just curious to see again what it was all about. Then too, sometimes he feels his idea of the work has drifted far from the thing itself: like any part of the past, stories are too easily reified. Picking up one of his books, starting to read, he has the shock of the familiar. A passage that gave him particular trouble, a story he'd almost forgotten, though, oddly, a single line can evoke much of the whole.

Leafing through the books: not to really read them. His eyes just won't do it. Often, however, he feels new insight into what provoked a given project. And though he may admire various lines or pieces, of course he can't help seeing what could have been done better. Even so, regret is usually short-lived. In part from a sense that he did what he could at the time ("But how can I picture it all?" Homer asks in the *Iliad*. "It would take a god to tell the tale."). In part from a kind of combined awe and fatigue at the thought of what it took to make the book possible. The relentless hunger for that particular project, for instance, a hunger long since gone. Then too the profane: calories consumed, all the hours, kilowatts. The most persistent emotional response, finally, is a feeling that whatever stories he has still to dream, he will not write those books again. No, they are foreign lands to which he once travelled, at some substantial cost. To which he can not, will not, return.

*They* were a good couple. Three fine kids, after twenty years still committed to bringing out the best in each other. She'd nearly always had at least a part-time job, only quit work when she finally decided to try to write the novel. She told her husband she thought it would take maybe a year.

Though more money never hurt, particularly with the oldest boy off at college, they didn't need the income from her job to survive. And since she'd talked so many times about trying a book, of course he wanted her to have the chance. On the other hand, now it had been nearly two years and still there was no end in sight. Therefore, he needed the writer's advice, had brought it all down to two questions:

1. How long do books take?
2. When is it no longer love to encourage someone to write?

L̄ake Como, the Alps. Tourists since before Pliny the Elder. (Playing the philistine, Mark Twain argued the relative merits of Lake Tahoe.) This enormous villa, bequest of Princess Ella della Torre e Tasso, nee Walker of the Detroit liquor family. Extraordinary vistas from the suite of each scholar-in-residence. Nazi pilots convalesced here; Mussolini was captured nearby. Coat and tie—or national costume—for dinner, *cameriere* pouring drinks out on the terrace. Olive, fig, grape. Gravel drives, paths. Lightning down the lake, thunder and the sound of churchbells from other villages carried up on the wind. Very black African economists striding through the topiary wearing Italian suits, Italian shoes.

Serious people of good will, the scholars work on their own projects, at mealtime joining to discuss the war in Lebanon, Reagan versus Mondale, World Bank policy, theater bibliograhy, schistosomiasis and the Aswan Dam, and, after a biologist's presentation, bluebird adultery / mallard rape / hummingbird prostitution. One Sunday afternoon there's a concert by a visiting pianist, another evening a lecture on nuclear winter and the imminent end of all life on the planet.

Joined one day by a large group of conferees from many nations, the scholars socialize according to post-Babel imperatives. What tribe are you? How many children? "Shakespeare," an enthusiastic young academician from Shanghai says, apparently having discerned a likeness, or, possibly, writer simply the first balding Caucasian author he's encountered live. "Shakespeare, I translate the language of English spontaneously." Beaming, the academician checks the list of scholars, reads the project description beside the writer's name: "A collection of short stories." "Shakespeare," he says, "please be so kind as to tell me. What kind of short stories do you collect?"

OFTEN, the writer has to fight the impulse to abandon a story. Not simply because its initial form and language are so sheer, but because the content disturbs. Too raw. Too true. Perhaps the writer also fears he's led himself astray. As Conrad put it, in the world of the book "there are no policemen, no law, no pressure of circumstance or dread of opinion to keep [the author] within bounds. Who then is going to say Nay to his temptations if not his conscience?"

Seamus Heaney speaks of the necessity of the artist to insist on "his own language, his own vision, his own terms of reference. . . ." To do so will "often seem like irresponsibility, sometimes like callousness, but from the artist's point of view it is an act of integrity, or an act of cunning to protect the integrity." Yes, yes. But then, as Robert Lowell wrote:

> I have sat and listened to too many
> words of the collaborating muse,
> and plotted perhaps too freely with my life,
> not avoiding injury to others,
> not avoiding injury to myself—
> to ask compassion. . . .

If fiction is risk, however, it is also opportunity. To go beyond sleep, beyond the unsayable, to define the human. Sometimes, the writer finds, as he works on the page a person is also being shaped, someone capable of measuring up to the stories being told. Perhaps this is part of what Chekhov meant when he wrote that his own life was the story of a boy who slowly squeezes "the slave out of himself drop by drop, and how, waking up one fine morning, he feels in his veins no longer flows the blood of a slave but that of a real man. . . ."

The craft skill here seems to be not to censor. To suspend judgment temporarily, if not longer. To learn to live with—to be!—what one has written.

◄ ◄ ◄

LE VRAI PARIS, late 1984. Right bank of the Seine, rush hour traffic congealed in the tunnel beneath the Louvre. Art and life. A kind of *son et lumière* just beyond, flics with long nightsticks, demonstrators rendering the Marseillaise, evoking newsreel footage of de Gaulle's triumphant return in 1945 until the eye discerns the fascist standards.

The writer and his French friend, trying to reach Place de la Bastille, returning from the Eiffel Tower, elevator having drawn them up and back as if by the nape of the neck. Terra firma down through the girders. A wobbling of knees. *Est-ce que vous avez le vertige?* School-children racing past on their way down, counting stairs.

"The worst thing I never saw," she says. "Some mans are coming." "He will be as us." Her English. The writer helps with idioms. "Happy as a clam." "Fuck a duck." "Cold as a witch's tit." "You drink like a fish." "I drink like a fish," she says, though she doesn't.

Up to his ears in French, savoring sounds. *Crétin. Épouvantable.* "*Les Anglais debarquent,*" she says. The British are coming? The redcoats are coming? Oh: her period has begun. "*Comme d'habitude, monsieur?*" the waiter asks, bringing coffee as the writer opens the *Herald Tribune.*

Busted on the metro. *Dans la merde.* Second-class ticket, first-class car. Her cat dips a paw into the creamer. Licks. Dips again. "*Bonjour, monsieur,*" the maid says. Tumescent in Paris. "*Quand je pense à Lénore, mon Dieu, je bande encore,*" Brassens sings. (And also, "*Mais quand je pense à Lulu, Là, je ne bande plus.*") The writer consults his pocket dictionary. *Bander,* to have an erection.

The basin of Enceladus at Versailles. His tiny hotel room under the eaves on rue Cardinal LeMoine. A Rumanian exile, friend of friends, in a cafe at Place Contrescarpe, his French fluent but spoken with a kind of Scottish burr, his perennial exasperation apparently rage at the loss of native tongue. *Loss of native tongue.* Now this gives the writer pause. English is his tongue. His medium. His instrument. Really, he is not himself without it. His French is functional, barely, no more. And though one can speak English in Paris, this isn't where English lives. And anyway, as Joni Mitchell sang it's "too old, and cold, and settled in its ways here." The writer wants—a McNugget. He wants to be there to hear the word enter the language.

The waiter wags his index finger, clucks his tongue, corrects as he informs: Too late for dinner. *"Merci,"* the writer replies, thinking Fuck You Too. And that, as they say, is one toke over the line. That tears it. Kiss my ass, ol' buddy, the writer says to himself. Kiss my English-speaking ass. Move it or lose it. Put the hammer down. Get back. Get outa my face. Ain't nothin' come to a sleeper but a dream. Hey, I'm goin' home.

P_HONE_ ringing, having neglected to pull the plug when he sat down at his desk, the writer stops typing. It's Richard, inspiration for—progenitor of—his character Mad Dog, calling from the booth on the corner. "Hey, mind if I come over?" This is an arrangement the writer has hammered out with him: Richard doesn't just show up.

Richard at thirty-nine, back from an appointment with his psychiatrist courtesy of the state of California, the Reagan administration, and taxpayers everywhere. "Real nice guy," Richard says. "Jewish from Newton Lower Falls. Tufts, then BU Med School. I told him I was getting homicidal again. I even gave him the diagnostic code: street Irish and crazy. He whipped the pills out in a flash." Richard wipes his mouth with the back of his hand, sets the bottle of Anchor Steam down on the wood stove. Sets it down hard, glass on iron. "Where'd you get that crap?"

"Coop liquor store."

"I know, 'Who made you come into my house when I was writing and pour my quality brew down your greasy throat?'" Richard laughs, takes out a dollar and places it on the stove. "Got another?"

"Jesus, Richard. It isn't water. What are you up to now? Two forty?"

"Two thirty, two thirty-five. Who gives a fuck?"

"Lynn doesn't mind?"

"She knews better than to volunteer her opinion, which is more than I can say for some people."

"You put on much more weight you'll get lost in there."

"I'm already lost in here. Where the hell am I anyway?"

The writer studies Richard. Where, indeed, has Richard gone? Now the head is massive, hair cropped. Jowls enormous, eyes closed. No neck. Tadpole, whale, torpedo.

IN 1983, Arthur Koestler, age seventy-seven, for some time an advocate of voluntary euthanasia, committed suicide with his third wife. In the last interview before his death, he said:

> Whenever I get depressed, which I often do, I come over here [to the bookcase]. . . . If ever I wonder what on earth it was all for, here is the evidence. The thirty books I've written plus all the translations. Forty-two different languages including English, Croatian, Ukrainian, Norwegian, Telugu. . . . I must have had something to say. There must be something in it after all.

In a poem Yeats wrote several years before his death, he appraises his life as a writer. After much hard work, "Everything he wrote was read, / After certain years he won / Sufficient money for his need. . . ." Friends, fame, family, all come to the poet.

> "The work is done," grown old he thought,
> "According to my boyish plan;
> Let the fools rage, I swerved in naught,
> Something to perfection brought";

Nonetheless, as at the end of each previous stanza, the voice of Plato's spirit is heard:

> But louder sang that ghost, "What then?"

"Richard, tell me something, what's the goal with all this weight?"

"Goal? There's no goal. Who said anything about a goal?"

"Come on. You've been crazy and violent for years, but now you can barely walk or breathe. Your arches are weeping. What standard of beauty are you measuring up to?"

"My father. My fucking father. He did the same thing. Late thirties, up eighty pounds. Beer. Food. Change of metabolism. No exercise. But underneath it all he was strong as a bastard." *Bahstid,* as Richard pronounces it with his Boston accent. "I called him the other night, actually. Told him to keep thinking of all those times he kicked the shit out of me and my brothers. A hundred times a year just for me, fifteen years before I took off. I'm not one of those liberal pieces of shit who forget about it. No way. I'm going to pull into Seabrook. Up in New Hampshire. He's working the reactor. I let him get a look at me, give him a big wave, drive off. So what if he calls the police? What are they supposed to do? I'm going to turn myself in after I get him. Shit, New Hampshire is easy time. I'm not going to kill him anyway. Just beat the living shit out of him. Then let it go to trial, have my sisters and brothers testify about what he did all those years. Humiliate him. Fucking slimeball."

Richard jumps out of the chair, incredibly light on his feet, as if his former self, star guard on the high-school basketball team, still defines motor movement. A moment later, whistling, he's back from the kitchen with another Anchor Steam, pulls out another single and places it on the stove. "So what were we talking about?"

"Your father."

"Fucking scumbag. He used to wait till you'd walk by, then cuff you on the back of the neck. Wicked fucking hard. Or wait till you were asleep. You never knew when he'd do it, just that he would. I sent him a Christmas card last year. One word, then my signature. 'Redress.' Let him look it up."

"Noun or verb?"

"Verb. As in, 'I am going to set the motherfucker straight once and for all.' You know, he could scare you shitless. After I jumped parole the first time, I must have been twenty-one, I called home from a bar in North Carolina. I'd been shooting hoops in the gym at Duke. 'Listen, Bucko,' he said when he heard my voice. I dropped the receiver, took off like a shot."

Suddenly restless, Richard jumps up again, heads into the kitchen, returns with another Anchor Steam, places another single on the stove. "Last one," he says. "No effect. I'm wired as a bastard." *Wired as a bastard:* a favorite phrase of Richard's, one the writer placed in the mouth of his character Mad Dog.

"The thin within," Richard says, downing the last Anchor Steam. "You know, inside every fat person there's a thin person struggling to break free. 'Help, I'm trapped inside this horrible body. Save me, please save me.' " Richard laughs, grunts as he gets up out of the chair. "Fuck it, I'm going to get some real beer. No more of this Yuppie shit. Anyway, you need to write. Get back to work. *Ciao* for now. Catch you later."

"Later," the writer replies as Richard slams the door behind him. *"Ciao* for now."

"THE stereotype of the successful American writer," argues John Hersey, "is one who with the slipping years becomes dissipated by a sense of failure, by literary politics, by alcohol, by envy, by praise or a want of it, by money or a lack of it." Certainly writing is a strange metier. "You're only as good as your last book," Mailer said. And no matter what the opinion of others, the writer knows that age may not bring greater power. As Paul Claudel wrote, "each new book involves new problems which make the experienced artist as insecure as a beginner—with the added difficulty of having to overcome the deceits of overfamiliarity."

On the subject of such hazards Hemingway perhaps earned the right to the last word. As he wrote in "The Snows of Kilimanjaro," "He had destroyed his talent himself—by not using it, by betrayals of himself and what he believed in, by drinking so much that he blunted the edge of his perceptions, by laziness, by sloth, by snobbery, by hook and by crook; selling vitality, trading it for security, for comfort."

WRITING about his mother's dying a year or so after her death, the writer had his doubts. Aren't some things better left unrecorded? Was this a kind of grave-robbing? Wouldn't he be invading her privacy, the privacy of his siblings? Thinking it over, he turned to his mother's volume of marriage poems, publication of which had come just after his father's death. A number of the poems addressed the issue of the beloved's relentless decline.

> I'm thinking you undone
> undiscerned
> minim by minim
> a corpuscle per day
> accomplishing descent
> by an easy gradient
> hardly numerable
> subtraction from yourself
> inclining so barely
> down massif aeons
>
> the bottom's no shock
> unless in my guile
> I counter your decline
> daily with a mounting
> need of you down
> one atom up two
> at the risk of finding
> you gone to the foot
> of the way with myself
> at the peak of want

Further, his mother had several times over the years said that one writes simply because one must. Her intent would have been to deflate pretension, but in this context the writer found it a consoling truism. And useful. He also reminded himself that there was no reasonable way to prejudge a story. Part of being able to write, it seems, inheres in just such bargains with oneself. Or just such self-deceptions. Whichever: he settled down to work.

To write about his mother's dying was also to write for the first time since her death. With the loss of a second parent, it more than once occurred to him, a certain story was over, a particular dialogue played out. Perhaps his books had been part of that dialogue. "I would have written of me on my stone / I had a lover's quarrel with the world," Robert Frost wrote. Perhaps the writer's quarrel had been at least initially with these two people, the first to love him, the first he loved. Exhausted after the months of his mother's illness, not yet reconciled to what he'd seen, he sensed that willy-nilly he'd been changed. Leaving him, perhaps, without the capacity to write / the desire to write / the need to write. Choose one.

In this period, struggling for balance, he read these lines in Howard Nemerov's *Journal of the Fictive Life:*

> . . . in middle life, you perceive as though suddenly what was always there to be perceived, that all the stories are only stories. Beyond the stories, beneath them, outside the area taken account of by stories, there are the sickbed, the suffering, the hopeless struggle, the grave. It makes the stories look like hypocrisy, and the vision is so terrible that one becomes grateful for the hypocrisy.

Grateful, finally, he began to write, though as it happened he set down fewer than two thousand words. In part, he considered these episodes enough to catch his mother's courage, their *lingua franca.* It was also true that to write more would force him to really take on those months again, and he just didn't have the heart.

These pages achieved, he waited until a very small book was published by Peter Howard and Poltroon Press. Five hundred copies not for sale. No title. Hand-set type. Hand-sewn. Now, the writer found, the text had new authority, seemed stronger than what he'd read over and again in manuscript, proofread in galleys. Pleased, he felt he'd been granted a force beyond his own, that he'd been playing an instrument it had taken millenia to evolve. With it, he'd commemorated something vital to him. And, in the words of Shirley Hazzard, in so doing had relieved his soul of incoherence.

Of course life goes on. About a week later, sitting in Peter's bookstore, the writer chatted with Jules, one of the regular customers. In his early fifties, a collector of Auden, Jules worked as a librarian at the university, had the air of being out of step with contemporary life and glad of it. He and the writer had spoken several times before.

"I read your little book this morning," Jules said. "I thought it really was quite good."

"Thank you," the writer replied, sensing that Jules hadn't finished.

"I liked it," Jules went on, "but I don't know. The thing is, I'm not at all sure I'd want one of my parents laid out like that for the whole world to see."

SHORTLY before he died, Bernard Malamud told an audience that if you keep writing for "years and years and years . . . ultimately you teach yourself something very important about yourself." According to the UP & AP account, "Asked what he had found out about himself by writing, Malamud said simply, 'I shall treasure that information,' and did not elaborate." One can, however, look to an earlier interview for some of what he might have added. Of writers who do only one draft, Malamud said, "They're cheating themselves." Asked what he would advise young writers, he said, "Write your heart out. . . . Teach yourself to work in uncertainty. . . . If you're not a genius, imitate the daring." Asked if, as some critics argued, narration is dead or dying, Malamud responded: "It'll be dead when the penis is." As for what writing had meant to him, Malamud replied, "I'd be too moved to say."

How's the book coming?
Is the book almost finished?
When do you think you'll be done with the book?

RICH in time, earning just enough to get by, he found that if he left himself nothing else he'd get to work. He cherished the slightly raffish freedom, the mix of bohemian self-indulgence and possible achievement. (As Deidre Bair describes it, Samuel Beckett tried to explain to his parents that "he wanted to be a writer, and that writing took enormous amounts of time during which it might appear that he was doing nothing.") Yet, though writing allowed him to set his own schedule, to be if not an outlaw then a kind of perennial undergraduate, in fact he wrote as hard as he could. In part because he craved work that seemed real, in part because only his effort stood between him and nothing at all. Reading about Colette's father, who apparently spent years in his study laboring on a book, the writer nodded ruefully to learn that after his death they discovered he'd written not a word. He also often thought of Carl Reiner and Mel Brooks's routine "The Two-Thousand-Year-Old Man." At one point, interviewer Reiner asks Brooks what the principal mode of transportation used to be. "Fear," Brooks replies.

Through completion of his third book, he seldom thought of himself as a writer. Nor did he have any sense of the shape of a literary career. He wrote a book. Saw it published. Did other things. Tried a second book. Saw it published. Rested. Read. Only slowly did he understand that few people really want not to do or to have something else. Regular income, more children, the reliable confirmation of others, weekends off. They want not to court autism for years at a time. Fair enough, the writer concluded. Surely there's no inherent virtue in writing. But a writer is also someone who writes. Clearly there was a kind of self-selection at work. Those who kept writing often received the serendipities that accrue to any persistent—or desperate—endeavor.

"Do you know that the final period of the book is an eye," he said, "and without lid?"
JABES, *Yael*

LIBELLI *habent sua fata*. Books have their own fate. Some authors, the writer learned when he studied literature in college, relied on the verdict of history to warrant their labors on the page. Often, tired of looking for love in the enormous reading room of Widener Library, the writer would wander the stacks, descending one level, then another, threading aisle after aisle of dusty volumes unread, untouched, for years. The writer went through college reading books, many of which had survived for centuries. Still, he thought, seeing the thousands of unread tomes, so much for posthumous redemption.

At forty-one, the writer for the first time heard himself speak of wanting to live forever. Not to avoid death, he was saying, or even the process of dying, but simply to have more time in this miraculous world. The writer was surprised also to note in himself a tendency to credit the young for what they possessed only inadvertently: youth.

Since then, the writer has divined this relationship between his own writing and immortality: that, once again deferring some imperative of adult life in favor of his work, he was in fact living as though he had all the time in the world.